THE STORY
OF THE SCRIPTURES

BOOK EIGHT

CHRISTIANITY IN ACTION TODAY

by

DAVID D. PRINGLE, B.A., M.Ed.

Didsbury College of Education, Manchester

Editor

M. E. J. SHEWELL, M.A., B.Sc., F.R.I.C.

SCHOFIELD & SIMS LTD.
HUDDERSFIELD

First Edition 1968
Reprinted (twice) 1969
Reprinted 1970
Reprinted 1971
Reprinted 1972
Reprinted 1973

PRINTED IN GREAT BRITAIN BY
HENRY GARNETT AND CO. LTD.,
ROTHERHAM AND LONDON

ACKNOWLEDGEMENTS

The author and publishers wish to thank the following for permission to reproduce copyright photographs which appear on the pages listed:

Roger Murray of The Christian, page 10.

Danilo Dolci Trust, pages 11, 12.

Fox Photos Ltd., pages 15, 109, 127, 131, 149.

The United Society for the Propagation of the Gospel, page 19.

Tom Wanless, pages 23, 117.

The Samaritans, page 27.

Miss Pat Thomas, A.R.P.S., A.M.P.A., page 30.

The Press Association Ltd., page 35.

N.S.P.C.C., page 39.

Christian Aid, by permission, pages 42, 44.

The Salvation Army, pages 46, 94.

U.N.E.S.C.O., page 49.

The British & Foreign Bible Society, page 53.

Oxfam; Martin Koretz; George Phillips, by courtesy of The People, page 56.

The Guide Dogs for the Blind Association, page 61.

Christian Medical College and Hospital, Vellore, page 65.

The Cheshire Foundation Homes for the Sick, page 70.

The Liverpool Echo, page 73.

Syndication International, page 77.

The Ockenden Venture, page 81.

Scripture Union, page 85.

By courtesy of the Gemeinde Oberammergau—F. Bruckmann, Munich, pages 89, 90.

Elsam, Mann & Cooper Ltd., page 97.

Shelter, page 101. Photograph by Penny Tweedie.

John Taylor, World Council of Churches, page 105.

W.R.V.S., page 114.

The Central Press Photos Ltd., pages 122, 155.

Scottish Field, page 136.

J. Allan Cash, F.I.I.P., F.R.P.S., page 139.

Keystone Press Agency Ltd., page 143.

Manchester Education Committee, page 151.

CONTENTS

CONTENTS

FOREWORD

If you have been using earlier books in this series you will know that four have been concerned with the study of the Old Testament and three with the New. This book, the eighth in the series, is concerned with the present and so we have called it *Christianity in Action Today*.

The contents provide an outline plan which will help you to find your way about the book more easily. You will notice that it has been arranged in three main stages, each covering one school term. Altogether there are thirty-eight separate topics : each is complete in itself and is followed either by questions or by suggestions for discussion, research or reading. The addresses of organisations and societies appear at the end of each chapter, and also in a longer list of "Useful Addresses" at the end of the book.

Term One begins by looking at Christianity in action in the lives of four individuals, and then goes on to show how it can grow and be strengthened through the work of groups of people, sometimes reaching national or even international proportions. In Term Two we see Christianity in action as a response to people's needs : sometimes those needs are physical, sometimes intellectual and sometimes spiritual — and very often they are a combination of all three. Finally, in the third section of the book, we see that Christianity in action is capable of changing people's attitudes to problems of all types — even, as the last chapters try to show, to those which exist within our own homes and families.

The individuals, groups and organisations mentioned in the book have been carefully chosen. Though the label *Christian* may not usually be attached to all of them, each of them, we believe, reflects in some way or other the spirit of Christ. But of course there are many other ways in which Christianity may work out when it is put into action, and many other examples might have been chosen. The work of youth clubs, and of the churches here and overseas, are two obvious instances.

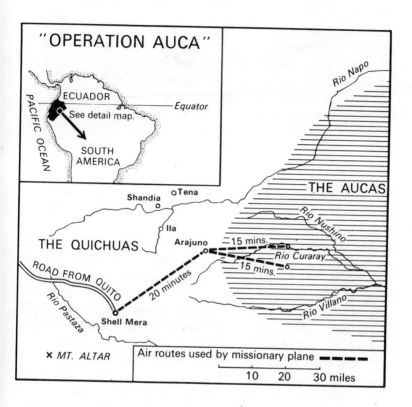

"OPERATION AUCA"

ECUADOR

PACIFIC OCEAN

Equator

See detail map.

SOUTH AMERICA

Rio Napo

THE AUCAS

Rio Nushino

oTena

Shandia

Ila

THE QUICHUAS

Arajuno

15 mins.

Rio Curaray

15 mins.

ROAD FROM QUITO

20 minutes

Rio Pastaza

Shell Mera

Rio Villano

× MT. ALTAR

Air routes used by missionary plane ▬ ▬ ▬ ▬

10   20   30 miles

1   NATE SAINT AND THE AUCAS

Hidden away within the jungles of Ecuador, in South America, live groups of Indians called Aucas. Until recently they were among the most savage and the most feared tribes on earth. Hating any invasion of their jungle privacy they would pursue any intruder until they could hurl their sharp, wooden spears at him. Only rarely did they miss their target.

Nobody knew exactly where the Auca villages were located and so the Aucas remained isolated, little known and greatly feared — until Nate Saint made up his mind to get to know them.

Nate had been a crew chief in the U.S. Army Air Corps during the war and when in 1944 at the age of 21 he decided to become a missionary, he joined the Missionary Aviation Fellowship. There was a growing number of small missionary stations in eastern Ecuador and Nate's job was to maintain contact between them in his small plane, The Pilot and to "lift" the missionaries when required into the most inaccessible parts of the area.

The more Nate heard about the Aucas the more curious he was to get to know them. His friend Ed. McCully, another young American missionary who had been famous at College as a footballer and athlete, was working nearby among the friendly Quichua Indians. Nate asked Ed. to fly with him over the neighbouring territory to see whether they could find the Auca settlements. Towards the end of their trip, the fuel nearly used up, they found a series of clearings and, as they flew lower, houses and signs of life. They came home greatly excited.

Making contact was another matter, however. To fly down and land in-one of those clearings would mean certain death. So, with the help of Ed. and two other young missionaries in the area, Pete Fleming and Jim Elliot, Nate arranged to fly once every week over the Auca settlements — high enough to miss the sure aim of the Auca spears yet low enough to drop presents and show that they wanted to be friends.

The scheme was elaborate. Nate designed a special fishing line with a canvas bucket on the end of it. A release mechanism enabled him to draw back the line into the plane. Using his skill as a pilot he was able to fly round in tiny circles and to lower that bucket without spilling its contents. The Pilot was almost as efficient as a helicopter !

Nate and Ed. dropped their first gift parcel on October 6th, 1955. It included a sack of precious salt, an aluminium kettle and twenty brightly coloured buttons for use as ornaments. The bucket was lowered with infinite care but there was no sign of the Aucas !

When the two returned to drop their next gift, a new axe, there was no trace of the first presents. This time, as the bucket was lowered, figures appeared outside some of the houses and one of the Aucas dived on the axe and seized it as soon as it reached the ground. The visits were kept up until one day, as the bucket was drawn back into the plane it was found to contain some wooden combs and a woven headband, presents from the Aucas to Nate and Ed.

The missionaries now judged that it was time to try to make personal contact. Early action was essential for the rainy season was coming and so it was decided to land early in January when it would be full moon. A fifth recruit, Roger Youderian, joined the team and a promising landing ground was found four miles from the Auca village.

On Tuesday morning January 3rd 1956 the five men met to pray together and just after 8 a.m. the operation began. Ed. McCully was landed first and then Nate ran a shuttle service until all the men and their supplies had been safely delivered. The next day Nate flew over the village with a loudspeaker inviting the Aucas to visit the missionary camp, but there was no sign of life. Thursday was equally disappointing but on Friday three Aucas were seen over on the other side of the river. Jim Elliot immediately jumped in and welcomed the man, woman and girl and all that day Nate and his friends entertained the Aucas in the camp, even taking the man for a flip in The Pilot. Now, they felt sure, the tribe would come over to visit them. But Saturday was as disappointing as Wednesday and Thursday had been.

Early on Sunday afternoon Nate decided to reconnoitre again and he returned very excited. Ten Aucas were coming along the river in the direction of the camp. Nate radioed his wife back at the home base, promised to make further radio contact at 4.30, collected his four friends and set off to meet the Aucas.

The missionaries did not live to send a further message. Some time that afternoon they were murdered by the tribesmen they had gone to greet. Subsequently their bodies were discovered and the plane and camp were found wrecked.

The story does not end there, however. The news of 'Operation Auca' was flashed around the world. More than a thousand students volunteered for missionary work when they heard the story of the courage of the five. More and more of the Indians living near the Aucas became Christians when they learned how Nate and his four companions had given their lives because of their belief in Jesus Christ.

But perhaps best of all, Nate's sister Rachel and Jim Elliot's widow Betty went back to live and work among the Aucas and gradually won their confidence. They have taught them to read and the photograph below shows two of them, Kimo and Komi on a recent visit to London with Rachel Saint.

Nearly everyone in the village from which Kimo and Komi come is now a Christian and they are able to help the missionaries in reaching the neighbouring settlements, which remain as hostile as ever to strangers.

1. Write or discuss what you think may have taken place in the last minutes before the five missionaries were murdered.
2. "In view of the many risks involved, Operation Auca was a foolhardy venture." Discuss this statement.
3. For further reading: *Jungle Pilot* by Russell T. Hitt, and *Through Gates of Splendour* by Elizabeth Elliot (both in Hodder Christian Paperbacks).

2   DANILO DOLCI

"A new Gandhi, a modern Saint Francis . . . " That's how one famous writer has described Danilo Dolci, a tall, powerfully built Italian who used to enjoy nearly all sports but now has little time for recreation.

Dolci was born in 1924 in a village near Trieste. His father was a stationmaster with the Italian State Railways and consequently the family moved about frequently. They were devout Roman Catholics. During World War II Danilo refused to enlist because Italy was a Fascist state and he was imprisoned. In 1943 he escaped and crossed into the Allied lines in the Abruzzi section of Italy.

After the war Dolci studied architecture and town planning for five years but he was not happy about the work and he did not sit his degree examinations. He also studied music at the Rome Conservatorio. Then for a short time he taught geometry and wrote poems, some of which were published. Yet it was not till 1950 that he began the sort of work he really wanted to do.

Don Zeno Saltini, a Roman Catholic priest, had founded a

11

village which he named Nomadelphia, within the shell of a German-built concentration camp just outside Modena. "Nomadelphia" is made up of two Greek words and it may be very roughly translated "how to live as brothers". It was intended that in this village orphans, and any adults who so wished, could live together and share their possessions in common, as had happened in the days of the early Christian Church. Dolci remained at Nomadelphia for two years until 1952 and then he went as a workman to the poorest, most miserable place he knew of — Western Sicily.

First he worked in Trappeto, a small fishing village, and then in Partinico, a poor farm town. He found men and women struggling amid utter poverty. He found widespread illiteracy and prostitution.

He saw fathers idle and out of work because employers found it cheaper to use child labour. Despite the fact that the Christian religion had long been established in Sicily, he found that the rule of 'an eye for an eye and a tooth for a tooth' still persisted. Injury was repaid by injury from one generation to another.

And behind all the poverty and misery, there was widespread fear of the dreaded Mafia. The Mafia, an outlaw organisation, had originated in Sicily in the nineteenth century. Estate owners, frightened by threats from the peasants, had paid groups of bandits to protect them. Despite several attempts to check it, the power and influence of these outlaws, who boasted about their contempt

Dolci (extreme left) leads a demonstration in Rome.

for the law, had grown. By the time the Second World War ended, the activities of the Mafia had spread through the industrial and business life of Sicily.

All these conditions preyed upon Dolci's mind. There was a constant drain upon public money simply to put down violence and disorder. The police were ruthless, and the law was openly defied. And then in 1952, in Trappeto, Danilo Dolci saw a child die of starvation.

Immediately he began his first public fast, designed to show up the problems of hunger in that part of Sicily and to expose the slackness of the government in dealing with it. After he had been fasting for a week Dolci had a thrombosis in his right arm, and a doctor wrote out a memorandum stating that he was dying. The next day a representative of the Prime Minister visited him promising immediate government relief for the desperate plight of that zone of Sicily. Dolci has since taken up the practice of fasting for at least a week every year!

In February 1956 the "strike in reverse" occurred. Dolci, angry and sick of the problem of mass unemployment, made his way with two hundred jobless men to a road outside Partinico which had become impassable through lack of repair. They spread out on both sides of the track and began working. After about twenty minutes seven truck-loads of police arrived armed with machine-guns, batons and tear-gas bombs. They stopped the project. Dolci and five others were arrested, charged and given a light sentence. The Chief Inspector of Police wrote in his report of the incident "Public order has been restored".

Dolci was on trial again in June 1957 for drawing attention in an article to sexual corruption in the slums of Palermo but his two months prison sentence was later cancelled by the Court of Appeal. Later in 1957 along with six others, he was awarded the Lenin Peace Prize. He pointed out very forcibly that he owed allegiance to no one political party and so he used the £9,500 prize money to set up "Centres for Full Employment" in five areas of Western Sicily. The aim of these centres is to help farmers improve their agricultural techniques. Though most of the work is done by local Sicilians a different national committee runs each of the centres and gives most of the financial help. The Swedes, the Swiss, the

13

Italians and the British each run one centre, whilst the Norwegians and the Dutch share responsibility for the fifth. During the summer season a good deal of work is done among children. The headquarters are at Partinico and contain a clinic, a good library and a hostel for the helpers.

The dogged determination of Danilo Dolci is beginning to show results. The government has been forced to give help in many of the most needy areas of Western Sicily. In February 1964 the feudal king of Sicily and acknowledged head of the Mafia, Giuseppe Genco Russo, was jailed. In other less dramatic ways also, Dolci has succeeded in cutting through the lengthy official procedures and State "red tape". But perhaps most important, the people of Sicily themselves are now beginning to show more real co-operation and initiative. Yet though Dolci numbers among his friends men of almost every nation, he continues to attract the anger and the hatred of many powerful Sicilians.

In many ways Dolci is an unusual man. Two years before he arrived in Trappeto he married the widow of a Trappeto fisherman who already had five children. Now he and his wife have children of their own — and they have adopted several more. It is reported that there are very rarely less than twenty children living in the Dolci household!

This eighteen stone giant with his rimless spectacles and clothes that always seem too small for him is no longer a member of the Roman Catholic Church — or, for that matter, of any other. Yet the self-sacrifice he has so often shown has led his biographer to describe his life so far as a modern fable — and he is not yet fifty!

1. "To know how to die is to know how to live." (Danilo Dolci) Do you agree with this statement?
2. For further reading: *Fire under the Ashes* by James McNeish. (Hodder & Stoughton 1965)
3. Write brief accounts about:
   (a) the aims and influence of the Mafia in the world today;
   (b) the new People's Centre at Trappeto in Western Sicily.
4. "Teaching people to help themselves is, in the long run, far more important than providing them with emergency aid." Write down your views on this statement and try to relate your ideas to the methods used by Dolci.

No society on earth is more multi-racial than that of the United States of America. It enjoys a higher standard of living than any other country. It is rivalled only by the Soviet Union in its role as a great world power. Yet its problems are manifold.

Many of these difficulties are, of course, external ones. But one of them, which in its own way is as crucial as any other, is an internal problem. It is the problem of the distinctions made between white and non-white. It is, in a somewhat different form, the same problem as that of South Africa. It is the problem of racial segregation.

For thirteen busy years, until his untimely death in April, 1968, Martin Luther King was right at the spearhead of the movement for 'desegregation' in America. A negro Baptist minister, he was blessed with endless patience and the determination to work, whenever possible, by peaceful means.

King was born into a comfortable middle-class home in Atlanta,

Georgia, on January 15th 1929. He had a 'respectable' background. His father and grandfather before him were Baptist ministers and his mother had been a schoolmistress before her marriage. Martin went to an all-Negro primary school and it was not till he was six years old that he discovered the "colour problem" in the form of two young white playmates whose parents then decided the time had come to discourage the friendship with the little negro boy down the road. He could recall also, in those early years, seeing members of the Klu Klux Klan beating negroes on the streets of Atlanta.

King had no thought at all of becoming a pastor when he began his studies at Morehouse College, Atlanta, which his father and grandfather had attended before him, but he was deeply influenced by his tutors there and in 1947 he was ordained for the ministry. He left Morehouse in 1948 with a B.A. degree to his credit and went on to a theological seminary in Pennsylvania where he obtained a B.D. degree in 1951. Further study at Boston and Harvard Universities followed and in 1955, still only 26 years old, Martin Luther King became a Doctor of Philosophy.

It was already obvious that he was no ordinary young man and when he took up his first pastorate in Montgomery, Alabama, he urged his church members to join the National Association for the Advancement of Coloured People. Events were soon to thrust him into prominence, for on December 1st 1955 a tired negro woman in Montgomery refused to give up her seat on a bus to a white person. She was arrested, and the result was a boycott by the negro community of all buses in that city which lasted for 382 days. The boycott was directed by the Montgomery Improvement Association — and the man they chose as their President was Martin Luther King.

From the beginning King was pledged to a policy of non-violence. Apart from Jesus Christ, the most powerful influence upon his life was Mahatma Gandhi, the great exponent of passive resistance. "From my Christian background," he once said, "I gained my ideals, and from Gandhi my operational technique." But there were many in the Civil Rights movement, as it has come to be known, who were constantly urging him to be more aggressive. When in January 1956 he was arrested for driving at 30 miles per hour in a 25 m.p.h. zone and when, four days later, his house was bombed, the negro community was ready for instant, militant action

16

But Martin Luther King pleaded with his followers for a forgiving attitude and an end of bitterness. His advice was heeded — and it paid real dividends, for from December 21st, 1956, negroes and whites have ridden together, unsegregated, on the buses of Alabama. Almost overnight Martin Luther King had become a national hero.

The movement which he championed gained ground rapidly and nearly every day brought its dangers and its excitements to the young crusader. At one time he was receiving as many as forty offensive phone calls every day as well as many letters threateni.ig the life of himself and his family. In 1958, about the time his first book was published, he was stabbed by a deranged negro woman but he went on, unshaken, taking a leading role in many demonstrations throughout the U.S.A. on behalf of desegregation.

Gradually, however, as his commitment to the Civil Rights movement increased, it became obvious that the routine tasks of his pastoral work in Alabama were proving a restriction. Early in 1960, therefore, he joined his father, Martin Luther King Senior, the minister of Ebenezer Baptist Church in Atlanta, Georgia, as co-pastor.

His work brought him more and more on to the international stage. In October 1962 he met President Kennedy and pressed for a firmer stand on Civil Rights issues. In August 1963, having by now gained wide support from many whites, he took part in a great march on Washington. On this occasion a vast crowd of 250,000, which included 60,000 white people, demonstrated in favour of the Civil Rights Bill at that time before Congress. The Bill was passed in 1964 and though it made substantial concessions Luther King did not believe it went far enough. Accordingly, in February 1965 Martin Luther King was in conference with President Johnson and Vice-President Humphrey and he stated afterwards that the President had declared his determination to remove the outstanding obstacles and injustices to the negro population.

King was a devoted husband and father. He lived near to the Church which he served in Atlanta. He was of medium height, fond of his food ("eating is my great sin," he used to say), a lover of sport and of visits to the opera. He was also a great speaker, not so much because of the techniques he used but because the sheer character and worth of the man shone through what he had to say. Like Winston Churchill he perfected the art of the 'cat-nap' which enabled him to sleep in a train or on a plane and so conserve his energies for the tremendous demands which were made upon them. He once said that almost always on occasions of great crisis he reached his decisions through prayer.

One of the greatest honours paid to Martin Luther King came in 1964 when, at the age of 35 he was awarded the Nobel Peace Prize. the youngest man ever to receive such a distinction. Characteristically, he used the 54,000 dollars prize money to finance Civil Rights activities.

A deep sense of shock filled the hearts of men and women when, on April 4th, 1968, the news of the assassination of Martin Luther King was announced to the world. He had been shot in the head whilst standing on the balcony of his hotel in Memphis, Tennessee, just a few days before he had planned to lead a march in support of the local dustmen, most of whom were negroes.

The processions, many of them completely silent, which were arranged throughout the United States and in many other countries bore eloquent tribute to the quality of a man whose life had often been compared with the life of Christ himself.

When his funeral service was over a farm wagon, drawn by mules, bore the body of this gallant Christian to Morehouse College, where he had begun his studies for the ministry, and there laid it to rest. Meantime, his struggle on behalf of all subdued peoples must be carried on by those who are left behind.

1. For further reading: *What Manner of Man* by Lerone Bennett (published by Allen & Unwin Ltd.).

2. "I hear not what you say, but what you *do* thunders so."
   Discuss this statement in relation to the four 'men of action' about whom you are reading in this book.

3. If it can be arranged, invite a coloured citizen to address one of your school societies about his experiences and impressions of Great Britain.

4. Speaking of the great movement of which he was a part, Martin Luther King once said " . . . it is a thrust forward to achieve something not just for negro people, but something that will save the whole of mankind."
   What is the "something", for which Martin Luther King worked and lived?

4   TREVOR HUDDLESTON:
"THE DAUNTLESS ONE"

Trevor Huddleston was thirty years old and already a priest of the Church of England when he set off for South Africa in 1943. He had been put in charge of mission work in Orlando and Sophiatown, two of the suburbs of Johannesburg, but when he arrived there he was shocked and staggered by what he found.

The South African government practises the policy of 'apartheid', or racial separation, between the negro and white sections of the population, and Orlando was being used as a *location* or area set aside to house Negro workers. Sophiatown, on the other hand, was one of the few places in South Africa where negroes were allowed to buy their own property. By 1949, however, its population was over 70,000 and it had become a *shanty town* so it was officially designated a slum. Huddleston's Church of Christ the King was in Sophiatown and he became deeply attached to its people. He was especially distressed by the under-nourished children, of whom he saw so many, and by the disease and the poverty of the people which all sprang from the policy of *apartheid*. It was certainly not easy to be a priest there, or to preach the gospel, because hungry people sometimes take what does not belong to them — and so large-scale stealing becomes an added problem.

Huddleston set to work in a very practical way. He raised enough money to build schools and nurseries for the negro children and for the construction of a first-class swimming pool in Orlando. He begged instruments for what became known as 'The Huddleston Jazz Band' and he got world-famous artists like the great violinist, Yehudi Menuhin, to give charity concerts. In 1945, with the help of European friends, he launched the African Children's Feeding Scheme. Though white children in South Africa got a free school dinner, negro children did not, but eventually the authorities agreed to provide school meals to coloured children at a very small cost and eventually, through the efforts of Huddleston and his friends, 5,000 negro children were being fed every day. In 1956, when he had been recalled to England, the South African authorities abandoned the scheme.

But Trevor Huddleston was becoming a marked man in South Africa and as its government tightened its grip upon the coloured peoples so his opposition increased. In February 1955 Sophiatown was demolished and the inhabitants moved to a new location eight miles further from the centre of Johannesburg. Huddleston opposed the scheme fiercely, accusing the government of violating the rights of the people. Further, he continually attacked the Pass Laws which required non-whites to carry passes at all times — and he helped many of his congregation when they were imprisoned for failing to observe these laws. On one occasion when a negro schoolboy was arrested after his pass had been deliberately destroyed by the police,

Father Huddleston intervened and was himself arrested. Later he received a special apology from the police authorities! Small wonder that he was known in Johannesburg as "Makhalipile", the dauntless one.

But he did not always receive support from those who might have been expected to give it. When the Archbishop of Canterbury visited South Africa in the Spring of 1955 he told Huddleston that he thought he was becoming too much involved in the politics of South Africa. Huddleston rejected the advice. Later he was quoted as saying "God is directly concerned in the way men behave to one another — that is, in politics."

Meantime the pressure against him was building up. The Prime Minister, Strijdom, called him a fanatic. Microphones were secretly installed in his house; his telephone was tapped and his letters opened. And then in the October of 1955, in the middle of a scripture lesson, he was interrupted by detectives who confiscated forty-four documents. It was clear that the government was going to take legal action against him before long.

In November 1955 the Community of the Resurrection, the religious society under which Huddleston worked, ordered him to return to England and he left in February 1956. The Prime Minister of South Africa is reported to have said, "Well, thank God, that's the last we'll hear of him! " A government official wrote to him, "If ever a man deserved to be drummed out of a country, to be ignominiously deported as an undesirable immigrant or, in the last resort, to be strung up from the nearest lamp-post as a renegade, it was you."

When Trevor Huddleston left South Africa he went first to the U.S.A. where he appeared many times in public, on radio and on television. In April he was back in Britain, making it clear that he believed South Africa should be expelled from the Commonwealth, and urging artists and athletes not to appear before segregated audiences. In that year also, 1956, came his book *Naught for Your Comfort* in which he tells of his experiences and of some of his hopes for the future. That book was branded as seditious in South Africa and seized by the police.

Though Father Huddleston remained in Britain from 1956 to 1960 his heart was really back all the time in Africa and few people

21

were surprised when in November 1960 he took up his work as Bishop of Masasi. He lives near to the Cathedral in a small African-style house which contains only a living room, a bedroom and a chapel. He spends up to two thirds of his time visiting ordinary people and the three hospitals and various schools for which he is responsible. It is usually to raise funds for a school or a hospital that he sometimes comes back to this country for a short visit.

His sense of humour, his simple manner of dress (usually open-necked shirt and shorts), his hard work and above all his devotion to Africa have endeared him to the African peoples. It was one of them, a student, who paid him perhaps the highest tribute of all when he said "I wish he were black."

———

1. For further reading: Trevor Huddleston in *Thirteen for Christ* by Alan Paton (Sheed 1963): Trevor Huddleston in *Workers for Humanity* by John Spencer (Harrap 1962).
2. Write a letter of encouragement from Huddleston, "exiled" in Great Britain in 1956, to the Church of Christ the King in Sophiatown.
3. "God is directly concerned in the way men behave to one another—that is, in politics".
   Do politics and religion mix? Discuss this question.
4. Trevor Huddleston returned to Britain in 1968 upon his appointment as Bishop of Stepney. Find out as much as you can about:
   (a) his work in this country;
   (b) his successor in Masasi.

5   ALCOHOLICS ANONYMOUS

Nearly everyone today understands what is meant by the term 'the affluent society' — and most of us, because our nation has become more prosperous, have been able to spend greater amounts of money on things which we enjoy. For many people this has meant the opportunity to drink more freely, and indeed, Britain's national expenditure on alcoholic drink has been greater in recent years than her expenditure on cars, motor cycles, radio and electrical goods combined. For most drinkers, 'social drinking' — that is, drinking in public houses or at home with friends, is something which is very enjoyable, something which is an important part of eir life. And most of them are wise enough to drink in modera-n : they know how to hold their liquor and they feel no insatiable iving afterwards for another drink . . . and another . . . and other.

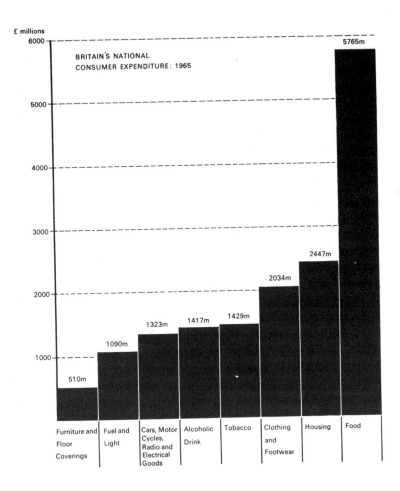

Some, however, have come beyond this stage. For them, the chemical composition of their bodies is such that it takes only *one* drink to change them into entirely different people, people to whom more alcohol is as necessary as is breath itself. They have nearly all passed through the preceding stages of controlled, social drinking to a point where they have lost the power to choose whether to drink or not. They are alcoholics, and alcoholism is a disease. Just as the diabetic dare not take sugar, so it is disastrous for the

24

alcoholic to consume alcohol. People like this must live as alcoholics until the day they die because there is as yet no medical cure for the disease from which they suffer.

It should, of course, be pointed out that only a proportion of heavy drinkers become alcoholics. Some medical experts have suggested that alcoholism, with its heavy craving for liquor, is an allergy. What is beyond doubt, however, is that the mental and physical condition of an alcoholic can deteriorate so seriously that he is as likely to die from his disease as is a cardiac sufferer from a heart attack.

Alcoholics Anonymous is an organisation which exists to combat this disease and the misery which it brings to the business and family life of those who suffer from it. Its many members in groups all over Britain and the U.S.A. have one thing in common — each of them is an alcoholic, and each of them knows that he is only one drink away from alcoholism.

It has been said that the problem of the alcoholic is centred much more in his mind than in his body. The Johns Hopkins University Hospital in Baltimore, U.S.A., has prepared a questionnaire designed to help those who are worried about their drinking habits to decide whether or not they are already, or are in danger of becoming, alcoholics. If they are, they can be put into immediate touch with a branch of Alcoholics Anonymous and there receive help and moral support from other people whose problem is the same.

Most people's impression of an alcoholic is of a down-and-out, tramp-like creature "sleeping it off" on a bench by the Thames Embankment. But many of those who ring up for information about Alcoholics Anonymous are professional people, often in influential positions and holding great responsibility — lawyers, bankers, teachers, doctors themselves — and sometimes ministers or priests. Not surprisingly, their religious beliefs are just as varied. As one of the booklets issued by the Association says :

"Every member of A.A. has his own interpretation and conception of God and religion, and the spiritual principles exercised in connection with his participation in Alcoholics Anonymous are those in which he believes and which he understands . . . . the only necessary concept to participation in Alcoholics Anonymous is your belief that a power greater than yourself exists and is much more capable of running your daily life than you have shown yourself to be."

The Association stresses above all in its work the importance of *today*. Yesterday is over and done with — tomorrow is not yet here : it is today which must be lived through in sobriety. Hence A.A.'s *Twelve Steps*, a list of resolutions which the alcoholic will read very frequently and in which he will admit his powerlessness over alcohol and again and again make a decision to turn his will and his life over to the care of God as he understands him.

Though more than 150,000 alcoholics have learned to give up alcohol through following the design for living which the *Twelve Steps* outlines, there are, of course, some who still slip back. It is to prevent this happening as far as possible that the local groups of Alcoholics Anonymous meet every week to discuss one another's problems, to reinforce one another's determination to stay "on the water wagon" and to organise aid for less fortunate alcoholics. Sometimes the group is "open" and relatives and friends are invited to join with the members : sometimes a preliminary group meeting is held for "beginners". There are no fees for membership of Alcoholics Anonymous — it is self-supporting through voluntary contributions but always, in case of urgent need, there is a telephone number to ring. And when the call goes through, it is more than likely that the receiver at the other end of the line will be picked up by another alcoholic.

---

1. Read *Prodigal Shepherd* by Ralph Pfau and Al Hirshberg (J. B. Lippincott Company, Philadelphia and New York 1958), the moving account of a priest alcoholic.
2. Find out all you can from the Ministry of Transport about the impact of breathalyser testing upon road accidents. Is such testing an interference with personal freedom ?
3. The Central Office of Alcoholics Anonymous, 11, Redcliffe Gardens, London, S.W.10 and the headquarters of Gamblers Anonymous at 19, Abbey House, Victoria Street, London S.W.1. issue pamphlets outlining their work and recovr programmes.

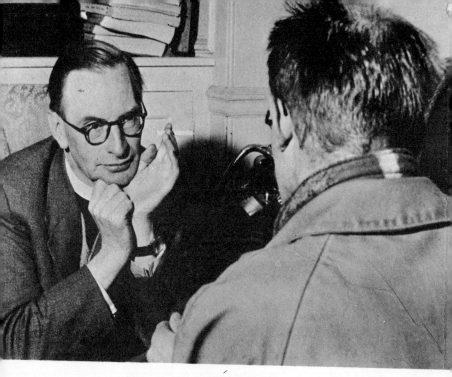

6

THE SAMARITANS

In Great Britain today about six thousand people commit suicide every year, and of this number roughly seven out of every ten give some indication beforehand of what they intend to do. Moreover, for every one who commits suicide, there are probably nearly ten times as many who attempt to do so but are unsuccessful.

The significance of these serious figures has been brought much more into people's minds in recent years by the Samaritans (often known as the Telephone Samaritans), an organisation which was started in 1953 by a priest of the Church of England, Chad Varah.

Chad Varah had been staggered to learn in the summer of that year that in the Greater London area three suicides were taking place every day; in other words every eight hours, week in, week out, a man or woman was dying by his or her own hand. Very much on impulse Varah made it known publicly on November 2nd 1953 that anyone contemplating suicide could get into touch with him by telephone. He had little idea that the service he was offering would be so eagerly received and accepted by so many men and women ! He had been greatly helped in finding a headquarters from which to operate by the offer of the Church of Saint Stephen, Walbrook, in the City of London. The patrons of that church, being sympathetic with his ideas, had appointed him Rector. Chad Varah also received valuable support for his scheme through publicity in the press, and later on radio and on television.

Today there are about 90 Samaritan centres in Britain in which telephones are manned day and night. These are centres which anyone 'tempted to suicide or despair' can contact simply by picking up a telephone and dialling an easily memorised number.

When a call is received in a Samaritan office the person who answers is usually a volunteer, just an ordinary man or woman who wants to help other people. And that means being prepared to *listen* patiently, for an hour or more if necessary. Most of the work which the Samaritans do is like this — undramatic, patient listening — and talking only when it seems really essential. Sometimes, however, the danger of suicide appears so serious that the 'Flying Squad' (usually two Samaritans in a car), will go out into the night and try to find the person in their home or on the street, or on a deserted railway station. Sometimes (in about one case out of every eight), it may be necessary to call in the specialised help of a psychiatrist. In most cases, however, an attempt will be made, once the immediate crisis is over, to bring in the caller for face to face conversation and further help in the offices of the branch. Often, especially in the large towns, the branch will be on Church premises, simply because this is usually the cheapest accommodation available in the centre of a great city. Usually, also, the Directors of Samaritan branches are clergymen, but it should be pointed out that no attempt is ever made to 'convert' those who ring up for help. And though the volunteers who staff the centres day and night are mostly attached to one or other of the main Christian denominations, some belong to other religious faiths and some have no religion at all. As Chad Varah has written, 'the only preaching the Samaritans are allowed to do is in deeds . . .'

Trainee Samaritans begin by attending preparation classes and after they have had some practical experience of observing actual cases they attend a series of further lectures. Each centre has its Director and its specialists — at least one medical consultant, usually a psychiatrist, along with social workers, ministers and so on. These experts are known as Leaders and it is they who usually do the counselling, whilst the volunteers are concerned with be-friending and offering practical help. If volunteers, by befriending callers, can 'put them on their feet' so that they become able once again to take up their work and leisure activities and to lead a full life, then their job will have been well done.

The whole of the Samaritan service is, of course, completely confidential. Yet it is interesting to note from statistics kept by the various branches that about three out of every eight people who ring up have serious problems connected with sex and that about four out of eight have psychological problems. Those who are classed 'serious suicide risks' are in fact about 10 per cent of the callers. Only about 2 per cent of those who phone are churchgoers.

The Samaritan idea has caught on quickly. In addition to the many branches in this country there are similar centres in several of the largest cities of America, throughout the Commonwealth, in Europe, in South America and South Africa. Each has its own particular methods of dealing with 'clients' but the main principles are the same — that someone is ready at the other end of the telephone to help and to befriend. And these volunteers, as Chad Varah has written, come 'in all shapes and sizes, of all ages and both sexes, from all types of background with all kinds of interests.' The organisation which he founded 'is prepared to scrap even the oldest tradition and jettison any method proved ineffective in serving the needs of the clients. Only one thing is sacrosanct . . . namely, to behave like the Good Samaritan in the parable towards those who are tempted to suicide or despair'.

1. "The only preaching the Samaritans are allowed to do is in deeds . . . " (Chad Varah). Discuss this statement.
2. For further reading: *The Samaritans—to help those tempted to suicide or despair*, has an introduction by Chad Varah. (Constable, London)
3. You are a Samaritan and you are planning to spend a day of your holidays with the person you are befriending. Outline your plans.
4. Either discuss or write about the implications of the fact that only about 2% of those who contact the Samaritans for help are churchgoers.

7   NARCOTICS ANONYMOUS

No single social problem in this country today receives wider publicity than that of drug taking and drug addiction. Narcotics Anonymous was set up to deal with that problem. It was started by amateurs because the professionals had achieved little success in dealing with it. It was set up with slender financial resources.

The pattern of drug taking itself is well enough known. Terms like "fix" and "pusher" have become part of the national vocabulary. A network of clubs in London and the provinces has provided a fertile market for drug traders and for the large syndicates within which they usually operate.

The facts about drugs themselves may be less familiar. The most dangerous category, *narcotics,* or pain-killing drugs are used every day in hospitals to relieve suffering. Morphine and heroin, two of the best known of them, are made from the juice of the opium poppy which grows in countries with a hot, dry climate, mainly in

Asia. The leaves of the South American coca shrub yield cocaine, used at one time by dentists to deaden the pain during extraction of teeth. The Indian Hemp plant provides the drug of that name which is also known as marijuana, hashish or cannabis. This drug is often distributed in the form of "reefer" cigarettes, sometimes being offered to "takers" without their being aware of the contents. The Home Secretary has reported that those known to be on heroin and cocaine are relatively few. However, the number of those using these drugs unknown to the authorities is probably many times greater.

This category of drugs is highly dangerous. Their continued use leads to symptoms such as loss of weight and appetite, defective muscular co-ordination, loss of concentration and often death itself. By law they must be kept under lock and key by authorised persons.

A second category, the *amphetamines*, comprise a large collection of more than sixty different drugs whose main effect is to stimulate the system. Some of them are commonly known as "pep pills", "purple hearts" or "black bombers". These drugs can be exceedingly dangerous if used in large quantities. Occasionally they have been known to circulate in schools, though it is an offence at law to possess them without authority. It is impossible to estimate accurately how many amphetamine addicts there are, though it is reliably suggested that the figure may run into hundreds of thousands.

A further group of drugs is known as the *hallucinogens*. One of them, LSD (Lysergic Acid Diethylamide) has been used in America under medical supervision to relieve mental anxiety. Another similar drug is mescalin. As the group name implies, these drugs produce hallucinations, many of which are extremely unpleasant. They can lead to suicide if they are used by people who are not emotionally stable.

It is important at this stage to distinguish between drug taking and drug addiction. It is true that some heavy drinkers never become alcoholics. It is true also that some young people who have taken drugs are able to avoid drug addiction. The startling fact is, however, that whilst it may take twenty or twenty-five years for a man to become a chronic alcoholic, serious addiction to drugs can come in two years or even less. It is significant, too, that the powerful men at the top of the big drug syndicates never take drugs themselves.

Most drug addicts are in fact people who have found the strains and stresses of modern life too great for them. They may have begun by flirting with drugs for "kicks", but they have quite quickly come to rely upon them as a means of lifting them out of, and away from, the next personal problem or puzzle which they have to solve. Whatever the reason for their involvement with drugs, however, the long-term effects of addiction are very serious indeed. From a physical point of view it produces damage to the heart and the brain. Almost always it leads to considerable changes in personality. It means a ruined career and, unless there is great sympathy and understanding at home, a broken family. It has no respect for persons or age. Old and young, men and women, boys and girls, doctors and nurses — we are all potential addicts.

If an addict is unable to obtain a further supply of the drug he has been using he will become very ill within a matter of hours, whether or not he is making a conscious effort of will to do without his next dose. He will suffer severe muscular cramps and bouts of pain in his arms and legs. He will be violently and frequently sick. These are the excruciating "withdrawal" symptoms which are as alarming to watch as an epileptic fit.

Narcotics Anonymous sets out to make sure that there is always someone from the organisation present with an addict during the painful withdrawal stages. It claims to maintain a twenty-four hour telephone service, though as yet its activities are mainly confined to the Greater London area. But its real work goes beyond those first agonising hours of emergency. It aims to establish with each addict a strong, personal relationship which may help him to get through the next trying days and weeks without further recourse to drugs. But it cannot yet function as Alcoholics Anonymous does. This is because the recovery rate for addicts is so low, and because so many who have believed themselves cured fall back again. It makes the work discouraging and of course it means that most of those who go to the aid of addicts go as amateurs, unable to enter fully into the experiences of the one they are trying to help. But these volunteers go also as friends — prepared to listen as well as to talk.

Narcotics Anonymous, though Church-sponsored, is completely inter-denominational. Its co-founder, Rev. John McNicol, is also the Secretary and founder of the National Association on Drug Addiction. Several voluntary bodies, including Narcotics Anonymous, have become affiliated with N.A.D.A. in a concerted attack on the drug problem.

The Government has done a little, but it could, and must, do much more in this field. As so often before in our national story, it is voluntary effort and voluntary organisation which have first tackled a social evil at the individual level. The organisation needs more money — and it can use many more helpers.

1. It may be possible to invite a representative of your local police force to talk to your year on the subject of drug addiction in your area.
2. Write for further information and, if necessary, advice, to: National Association on Drug Addiction, 9, Anchorage Close, London, S.W.19.
3. Do you believe a professing Christian is any better fitted to offer help to a drug addict than someone who claims no religious belief?
4. "Drugs or no drugs, my personality's my own—to do with as I like." Do you agree with this statement?

8 ABERFAN

There has never before been anything quite like Aberfan. For decades the people of Wales have lived with the threat of disaster — of a collapsed coal seam or a blocked shaft entrance — over their heads. Women and their children have stood many times at the pit-head waiting for news of husbands and fathers, brothers and sweet-hearts trapped below. Often the tragedy has been overwhelming, and the names of the great colliery disasters are stamped upon the hearts of generations of the Welsh people.

Aberfan was different. Now it was the men and women who worked and waited . . . for children.

The crude, stark facts of those nightmare days and nights are well enough known. On Friday morning October 21st 1966 a vast tip of slag, perched high over the village of Aberfan in Glamorgan-shire, began to move. A crane driver and some of his mates noticed about 7.30 a.m. that the top of the tip had sunk by about ten feet. Part of the crane had disappeared into the tip. One of the men went off down the mountain-side to report to colliery officials because the telephone wires linking the top of the tip with the colliery had been stolen.

By 9 a.m. the head of the tip was about twenty feet below its normal level. The workmen became perturbed and went off to confer in a nearby shed over a cup of tea. Then suddenly, with a noise which has been described as that of a jet aircraft, the tip poured in a rolling wave down the side of the mountain. It engulfed two cottages, a row of terraced houses, and Pantglas Junior School — and it went on advancing, inch by inch, for many hours longer.

The descriptions of the disaster as they have been recounted by those who witnessed it are grim and harrowing. Chaos was every-where. Slime and mud and torrents of water from the tip, and later heavy rain, conspired to confound the efforts of those who worked.

Help began to pour in almost immediately. An official estimated that there were 254 children on the school register and that 91 were

safe. Teachers began passing some of the rescued children through classroom windows which they had smashed. The battle to free the three trapped classrooms with pick and shovel and bucket began. Bulldozers were soon at hand but they could not be used near the stricken classrooms. Soon the first bodies were freed, put on to stretchers, discreetly covered and passed into waiting ambulances. About 11 a.m. two badly injured children were rescued and spirits soared as it seemed possible others might be found alive.

In the streets of the village nearly all the doors were open. Sheets and blankets, food and shoes, plates and cups were passed out. The Salvation Army set up a mobile canteen. The Baptist chapel became a casualty and refreshment centre. A temporary mortuary had been opened but already it was too small and another Sunday school, Bethania, was taken over for this purpose. Nurses, policemen and Red Cross workers washed the bodies before they were taken into the Church for identification. Fathers and mothers queued outside in the street throughout that Friday night, wondering whether their children had yet been found.

The reality dawned quickly upon the world outside. There was full press and television coverage, much of it brilliantly and most sympathetically done. In a situation which really defied description, words were somehow found through which listeners far from Aberfan could share, by thought and by prayer, in a national disaster.

By Sunday evening 138 bodies had been rescued and of that number 118 had been identified. Many were angry as they remembered the protests which parents had made earlier in the year about the mud and the water through which their children had had to pass before they could get to school. Little, it seemed, had been done by officialdom to heed the warning signs and to act upon them. The Mayor of Merthyr Tydfil, nearby, launched an Aberfan Disaster Appeal, but it could not bring back the lost children. Nor, for that matter, could the Government Inquiry which it was announced Lord Justice Edmund Davies was to head.

Arrangements were made for a communal burial service to be held on the Thursday, and so most of the funeral services were held on the Wednesday evening in the chapels and the churches which the children had attended. At the mountain-side cemetery two huge trenches, each eighty feet in length had been dug to receive the coffins. A cross more than 100 feet tall had been made out of the flowers sent from men and women all over the world. When the Queen visited Aberfan eight days after the disaster she was informed that 144 people had died. Of those, 116 were children. The Headmistress of Pantglas Junior School, the Deputy Headmaster, three teachers and a part-time clerical assistant had all perished.

The Government Inquiry will have been worthwhile if it has ensured that another Aberfan never occurs in Great Britain.

The vast sums of money contributed to the Disaster Fund are an indication of the impact which this tragedy made upon our national life. Yet it is the small, apparently unimportant things which make Aberfan memorable. One remembers, for example, how people stood in silent prayer in a bingo hall in the Midlands on the night of the disaster. One recalls the many thousands of letters and telephone calls in the days immediately afterwards, assuring the stricken village that prayer was being offered by ordinary people all over Britain. One thinks of services like the one by the open communal grave, in which the differences between denominations no longer seemed to matter, and of a chapel's communion table covered, not with bread and wine, but with bandages and antiseptic. Nor does Aberfan forget the offers of free holiday accommodation, both at home and abroad, for the bereaved families and the surviving children, or the thousands of toys which poured into the village.

A whole army of people, many of them themselves bereaved, had simply done what they could, regardless of the cost in terms of time or treasure.

Faith wavered and faltered during those days of late October. Yet despite the anger and the bitterness, the tragedy that was Aberfan released a whole torrent of loving kindness which was never more evident than when the situation appeared to be at its worst. Words, indeed, were of little use, but action — "the language of love" — as Edward England has written, this was what surrounded and encompassed Aberfan.

---

1. Read *The Mountain that Moved* by Edward England (Hodder & Stoughton 1967) for a day by day account of the course of events at Aberfan.
2. When Edward England asked a Muslim his opinion of the Aberfan disaster he replied "An act of God. Earthquakes, floods, typhoons, all come from God". Discuss or debate his reply.
3. "Never has the essential unity of the Church been so effectively demonstrated. All talk of denominations is quite irrelevant. The team of clergy and ministers act as those who belong to the one Church of Christ." (Dr. Maldwyn Edwards, a Methodist Minister, visiting Aberfan). How might the co-operation secured during a terrible emergency become 'the order of the day'?

Americans sometimes tell us that we in Britain place a higher value on our animals than we do upon our children ! The Society which deals with cruelty to animals, they remind us, is a Royal Society (R.S.P.C.A.) — the parallel work amongst children rates only as a National Society.

It is difficult to say whether there is any truth at all in these remarks, yet it is interesting to note that growing anxiety about the sufferings of children first took practical expression in the U.S.A.

A Liverpool banker, T. F. Agnew, came home from a visit to America much impressed by the work of the New York Society for the Prevention of Cruelty to Children. It was largely through his persuasive efforts that in 1883 the Liverpool Society for the Prevention of Cruelty to Children held its first meeting. It was the first society of its kind to be set up in this country. In the following year a similar society was formed in London. Lord Shaftesbury was its first President and the Rev. Benjamin Waugh, a Congregational minister, was Honorary Secretary. In 1889 the work of several similar societies was brought together as the N.S.P.C.C. and Waugh became the first Director.

Since those early days a tremendous amount of work has been done. Parliament has passed legislation dealing with children. It has sometimes extended it, sometimes amended it and periodically codified it. But the law concerning children is now clear, and the N.S.P.C C. knows precisely when to intervene in the affairs of a family and when not to do so.

Since 1884 the Society has dealt with nearly three million cases of cruelty and it continues to cope with between thirty and forty thousand new ones each year. About two thirds of these are brought to the notice of the N.S.P.C.C. by ordinary people whilst the rest are reported by the police, school officials or by the Society's Inspectors.

The great majority of the cases can be dealt with either by warning or by advice. In less than one case out of every hundred, however, the Society prosecutes the parents. Sometimes, also, children or young people are brought before the Juvenile Courts, which generally means that they are thought to be in need of care and protection. They can then be committed to the care of a local authority or some other fit and responsible person.

About two thirds of the work which the Society has dealt with over the years has been concerned with neglected children. Neglect

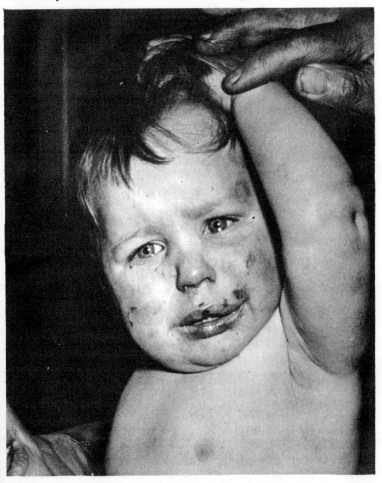

may occur for a variety of reasons. It can sometimes be due to the low intelligence of parents. It may be caused simply because a mother becomes increasingly overwhelmed by the demands of a constantly expanding family. It may be worsened by the poor health of one or both parents or by the father's unemployment. Yet the cold facts remain. The N.S.P.C.C. deals with rather more than 20,000 cases of neglect each year — and most cases, of course, involve more than one child. The following account of a visit paid to Mrs. A's home is fairly typical :

'There are empty detergent and cereal packets piled amongst empty tins whose scrapings are congealed and mouldy; newspapers, some of which have been used as toilet paper, fill crevices between empty, soured milk bottles, a profusion of cigarette packets and rancid margarine papers. Soiled sanitary towels, orange peel, clothes stiff and grey with dirt and a mass of unidentifiable rubbish complete the picture . . . . The next room is similar except that there is evidence of cooking around a poor type paraffin stove; cold grease in a frying pan lies next to a chamber pot full of urine and excreta, and bluebottles appear to find both an ideal breeding ground. The whole collection of human and material rubbish is covered with a miasma of dust and a stench which defies description.

Some thousands of cases reported to the Society each year come under the heading of "physical or mental cruelty". How many more remain undiscovered is not known. Certain it is that many adults, fully aware that physical ill-treatment of children is going on around them, refuse, for fear of 'getting involved', to inform either the N.S.P.C.C. or the police. The story of a little girl named Katie may help to illustrate the sort of problem which the Society has to face.

Watching from a neighbouring bedroom window :

'The doctor saw a thin eight-year-old girl standing absolutely still, except that she was rubbing her hands together in endless little washing motions. Her face was blue, her coat torn. The small patch of grass on which she stood was worn away and joined by a tiny strip to another equally small square of bare earth. Only between these two spots in the garden was the child allowed to move. This had been going on for nine months from eight in the morning until six at night, whatever the weather. . . . She stood there while rain lashed down and filled her shoes, whilst the earth was frozen hard and snow lay in its cracks, and whilst the intense June heat made the day unbearably hot . . . . She was neither fed nor allowed to use the lavatory during her hours in the garden . . . . Neighbours had passed apples and biscuits through the fence to her and they had seen her standing naked in the bathroom every evening when she was taken in, washing her inevitably wet and soiled clothes. *But they had not informed either the N.S.P.C.C. Inspector, any other social worker or the police.* And, since a further row of houses backed on to Katie's . . . . it seems likely that as many as thirty or forty adult people were aware that a child was being cruelly ill-used.'

But there is a brighter, happier side to the Society's work too. Nearly thirty per cent of cases occur because mothers and fathers themselves come to the Society for advice about themselves and their children. Perhaps a woman is in arrears with her rent and unable to straighten out her affairs. Sometimes it may be that the father of a large family has been imprisoned and the mother is anxious and worried about the management of the household. Sometimes it is children themselves who come to seek help and advice on behalf of their parents.

No praise can be too great for the sympathetic work and interest of the N.S.P.C.C. Inspectors and Women Visitors. They are recruited with a wide variety of previous experience. Some men come to the N.S.P.C.C. after a career in the armed forces, but others are brought in for a year's training, from industry, the police and the prison services and from teaching. Their work is fascinating in its range and opportunity. It is done in a variety of ways, too numerous to mention in a short survey of this type. But it is *always* done if it appears that children are in real need or danger.

———————◆———————

1. Read *This is Your Child—the story of the N.S.P.C.C.* by Anne Allen and Arthur Morton (Routledge and Kegan Paul 1961) from which the two case histories quoted in the chapter are taken.
2. " . . . there does seem to be a real feeling amongst social workers and local government officials that rejection of children *within their own home circle* is on the increase." (*This is Your Child*, page 125.) Discuss the implications of this statement and, if you believe it to be true, suggest some possible reasons for it.
3. The N.S.P.C.C. has a junior section, the League of Pity, and up to the time they leave school all boys and girls are eligible to help with its work. Find out all you can about the League and then, using not more than 750 words, write an account of its activities.

10   THE MASAI SCHEME

There is a larger British community in Kenya than in some of the other African countries and that is perhaps one reason why it is often in the news. The story of the Mau Mau and the terrorism which led to widespread bloodshed and tragedy was front page news in English newspapers for nearly five years. Now Kenya is in many ways more settled and some, at any rate, of its problems seem less complicated than they did a few years ago.

Many areas of Kenya are extremely beautiful and in some parts it has a perfectly balanced climate. The Masai tribesmen, about

30,000 in number, live in a wide arc of undulating grassland to the south-west of Nairobi. They are a nomadic people, living an un-hurried, pastoral life and with a strong sense of community and a love of tradition. They have always lived almost entirely on the produce of their cattle (milk, blood and a little meat) and they have allowed the beasts to graze in large herds over a very wide area. Since they have been loath either to kill or to sell their animals, there has been a progressive deterioration in the quality of the cattle. Many, also, were lost through serious drought and floods a few years ago and the number of beasts fell from about half a million to approximately 200,000. This drastic reduction in the number of stock made it imperative for the Masai to turn to other sources of supply for their food. Yet they were reluctant to alter their long-established habits and resisted efforts to change their way of life.

Then the Christian Council of Kenya put forward an ambitious agricultural and nutritional project for Kenya as a whole, and included within it was the proposal to set up a Rural Training Centre for the Masai people.

The Kenyans themselves were unable to finance these proposals and so help was asked of the Inter-Church Aid Division of the World Council of Churches in Geneva. After careful examination the Masai project was approved. In due course the British Council of Churches, which is affiliated with the World Council of Churches, was informed of the scheme and one of its member branches, the Manchester and District Council of Churches, decided to make the Masai its special concern.

Councils of Churches are made up of representatives of nearly all the main Christian denominations except the Roman Catholic, and most people are now familiar with Christian Aid Week which is usually held each year in May, and with the small envelopes which are pushed through doors and later collected. The Manchester Council has been supporting the Masai scheme for several years now to the tune of about £10,000 annually. Much of this amount, though it is not the full cost of the project, has come from the con-tributions of many Christians and non-Christians during the various Christian Aid weeks.

The work which has been done among the Masai people is impressive. Buildings once used as a Mau Mau detention camp

43

have been adapted to house a primary school, a tannery and rooms in which leather-craft can be taught. Another part of the camp has been converted into College buildings in which teachers, students and workers can live and study. A series of six month courses in the methods of settled farming are arranged for young Masai (usually from the Moran or Warrior class and aged between about 18 and 28), and three-week courses are laid on for ranchers. A cattle enclosure, giving protection from wild animals, has been built and trial plots of high-yielding grasses such as Napier grass and Guinea grass have been planted. Vegetables and maize are growing apace and a piped water supply has been provided to serve much of the region. A distillery has been built where an insecticide is manufactured for spraying cattle against ticks, which are carriers of coastal fever.

The tannery has been particularly successful. Here excellent quality goods are produced, both for export and local sale and the

present turnover is of the order of £120 per month. Several head of cattle of first-class calibre have been acquired and in October 1966 the Centre sold its first 'home-bred' beasts, all of Grade 1 quality, to bring in an income of £3,000.

Although the large-scale help from the Manchester and District Council of Churches was planned to end in 1968 there seems to be a good chance that Manchester will go on helping on a smaller scale.

The task of bringing new approaches and methods of farming to a poverty-stricken area of Africa has been a long-term one, but already it appears to be yielding exciting results. A young Masai agriculturalist of great promise has been appointed Vice-Principal of the Training Centre and when the Principal, an English Agricultural missionary, goes on leave he is able to assume full responsibility for the project.

In the words of Kenya's Prime Minister, Jomo Kenyatta, the Masai scheme is providing 'the means to give long-term help and permanent freedom from hunger to many people.'

1. Using not more than 300 words in all draw up, and if possible illustrate a leaflet which explains the Masai scheme and would be suitable for door-to-door distribution during Christian Aid week.

2. Obtainable from Christian Aid at 10, Eaton Gate, London, S.W.1 are a variety of study guides including *World Poverty and British Responsibility*.

3. "We have forgotten that the first petition in that part of the Lord's Prayer which relates to man is not about forgiveness, or about temptation, but 'Give us this day our daily bread . . . .' We excuse ourselves by saying that 'man shall not live by bread alone' and use it as a sop to conscience as we preach religion and pursue policies which deny bread and life to hundreds of thousands". (Baptist Times). Discuss this statement.

11   THE SALVATION ARMY

When William Booth and his wife Catherine left the Methodist Church in 1862 it was because fellow churchmen were suspicious of their 'revivalistic' methods. Most churches of that day were opposed to anything which appeared to be an unusual or unorthodox approach to the preaching of the Christian gospel. For two years, the Churches closed against him, Booth, who had been accustomed to addressing great congregations, wandered about the country preaching only to handfuls of people in the smallest of buildings. Then, in 1865 he began to hold preaching meetings in the streets of the East End of London and in tents, music halls, theatres and so on. His following was soon great, for his direct, uncomplicated way of speaking made a great appeal to ordinary people. The "East End" of that day was almost incredibly squalid and filthy. On its fringe, however, it carried shops and some better houses, and it was principally from this particular area that William Booth's first helpers in his "Christian Mission" came.

From the very first the work had its practical and social side. Booth had "a profound pity for the outcast and a hatred of dirt, squalor and suffering". He knew it was a mockery to preach to men and women when their stomachs were empty. The soup kitchens, the free breakfasts, the 240 tickets for bread and meat which the Mission was able to distribute every week to needy people, the rescue work amongst women and the night shelters — all this and much more was made possible by the voluntary subscriptions of interested supporters throughout the country.

In 1878 the mission was re-organised on a military basis and the title "The Salvation Army" was adopted in 1880. William Booth modelled his "Orders and Regulations" on those of the British Army. Unquestioning obedience was required throughout all the ranks and the organisation was, and remains today, autocratic. Booth himself, as the first General, was its undisputed leader until 1912.

In 1880 work began in the United States and in 1881 in Australia. Gradually also, in this country, perhaps because of the active support of King Edward VII, the sincerity of the motives of Booth and his followers was recognised. Despite the fears of some supporters, adherents continued to increase in number in the years immediately following the founder's death in 1912. In 1918 the government gave its first subsidy to the Salvation Army for maternity work.

The variety and scope of the work of the Army today almost defies description. It is currently working in seventy countries and preaching is carried on in 146 languages. Settlements for criminals have been established in India and leper colonies in the Dutch Indies. Wherever possible converts are set to work at once with a definite job to do. They are also encouraged to testify in public concerning the changes in their lives which have accompanied their conversion.

The Salvation Army remains direct and practical in its approach. It asserts the reality of sin, and it refuses to be side-tracked into finding comfortable excuses to explain away its effects in the modern world. And despite increased national prosperity and affluence, it has continued to uncover cases of poverty and need.

In 1965 the Army fed more than two million people at its food distribution centres. More than 24,000,000 meals were served in its 521 hostels for homeless people. Over a quarter of a million prisoners were visited and the Homes for Alcoholics, the Eventide Homes and the Homes for Unmarried Mothers continued their vital work. The specialised activities concerning missing persons were carried on, nearly 14,000 enquiries being followed up and 6,500 people traced.

From an early date music has played an important part in the

Salvation Army's work. William Booth contended that there was no such thing as 'secular' music and the familiar, uniformed brass bands have brought listening groups of people to the street corners for many years now. But where some of the Churches have been nervous of the electric guitar and the 'pop' medium, the Army has not been afraid to use them. The "Joystrings" (a group of young Salvationists) made music in the modern idiom and they made it capably and professionally.

Great use has also been made of the printing press. The Army newspaper, the "War Cry", first published in 1879 continues to appear each week and is widely distributed throughout the length and breadth of the land.

A complex headquarters organisation in London co-ordinates the Army's work throughout the world. There are, amongst others, Finance, Literary, Overseas and Public Relations Departments and the principal administrative posts are held by commissioned officers of high rank. Yet irrespective of status in the Army, all officers accept a relative poverty and are only paid what is necessary for their basic needs. Women have from the very beginning enjoyed absolute equality of privilege, position and dignity in the Salvation Army and for a time William Booth's daughter, Evangeline, was the General.

The Salvation Army has come in for its due share of ridicule and abuse. It has generally been glad to receive it, if only because its existence and its work have thereby been brought into the forefront of people's minds. There are few, however, who have seen the Salvation Army in action in the "front line", whether in a war theatre or at a disaster such as Aberfan, who will hear any serious criticism levelled against it.

1. Read *The Salvation Army Year Book*, available in most public libraries, and then write an account of the scope of Army work overseas.
2. " . . . it would have been little short of calamity had William Booth not been forced out of the Church to become founder of the Salvation Army." (From Volume 1 of *The History of the Salvation Army* by Robert Sandall.) Discuss this statement.
3. Find out all you can about the work of the Salvation Army in your area and write a brief report about it.
4. "Sin is real!" What is sin? How do Christians fight it?

12
UNESCO:
MAKING THE WORLD LITERATE

There has been a great deal of emphasis in recent years upon the need to feed a starving world. What we know already about the Masai scheme and shall later find out about Oxfam shows us that the emphasis is right. It is of course absolutely true that it is no use trying to teach a man how to read if his stomach is empty and likely to remain so. Obviously the first priority must be food to prevent him from starving.

It is equally true, however, that the greatest help which can be given to a hungry man, once he is adequately fed, is to show him how to combat hunger and how to earn his own living. Material assistance can relieve famine and drought, but food and water given for an emergency cannot prevent a similar situation from occurring again. Only education — and that, in the first place means literacy — can equip a man to think for himself and to plan his future.

Over the last twenty years there has been a series of experiments to combat illiteracy and UNESCO has been behind many of them. UNESCO—the United Nations Educational, Scientific and Cultural Organisation, is one of the agencies operating under the United Nations Organisation. It is pledged 'to free mankind from illiteracy, advance the spread of scientific knowledge and increase international understanding through the exchange of education and culture'. Its headquarters are in Paris.

Reliable estimates inform us that there are at least 700 million illiterate people in the world today, and probably very many more than that. At the time of writing this chapter the population of the world is about 3,500 million. That means that at least a fifth, perhaps even a third of the world is unable to read.

The efforts made by UNESCO and by others have produced a decline in the percentage of world illiteracy. Nevertheless the population explosion has been so rapid that the actual number of illiterate people is still increasing. Mass illiteracy is worst where economic conditions are poorest and where average incomes are lowest. In today's world that means principally Asia, Africa and Latin America.

At this point it is probably wise to explain precisely what is meant by the term "literate". The fact that you are able to read and understand the words in this book, and perhaps to work through the suggestions at the end of each chapter shows that you are a highly literate person. Literacy, then, in its fullest sense means the ability not only to read and to write but to reason and to argue from what has been read or written. It is obvious that it would be well-nigh impossible to achieve this goal in world terms, and so the term "functional literacy" is used. This means more than just making out the letters on a printed page, yet less than literacy in its fullest sense. As used by UNESCO it means that a person is able to read a newspaper or to follow simple instructions, to write a simple letter and to do simple accounts.

The problem of literacy is not, of course, confined to children. Millions of children who never learnt to read at all have grown up and are now adult. Some are still young, some middle-aged whilst others are elderly or old. For all sorts of reasons these men and women deserve to be given the chance to read. They deserve it because, as UNESCO says "literacy is the key that unlocks the door to the future". It enables a man to think for himself and to challenge the truth of what others tell him. It enables him to be a more intelligent parent and to do exciting things in his spare time. It gives him the chance to improve his economic position. Equally important, it makes him a more efficient worker.

It is not surprising that Lenin referred to illiteracy as "Enemy Number One". When he gained power in Russia, a nation-wide campaign was mounted to wipe out widespread adult illiteracy. Twenty years later that target had been largely achieved.

It is good to know, therefore, that today men and women all over the world are being reminded that it is never too late to learn to read. Sometimes it is a government which is pioneering the literacy campaign. More usually it is a voluntary organisation, often a missionary society or trade union, which is doing the work. But frequently UNESCO staff are on hand to advise and guide local efforts.

The money at the disposal of UNESCO is very limited when compared with the immensity of the problem which it is tackling. Consequently, the Organisation plans its work almost like a military operation. It must make sure that those who are in charge of local campaigns against illiteracy are as skilled as possible. Therefore there are experts to advise governments in planning their strategy. UNESCO scholarships are awarded to talented people who are fighting illiteracy in their own lands. The scholarships enable them to travel, to do research and perhaps to attend a university for a time. UNESCO also arranges courses and conferences so that local pioneers can meet with one another and share common problems.

Those problems, of course, are many. Almost everywhere in the world today teachers are in short supply. Often it is necessary, therefore, to use people without professional qualifications to teach adults how to read. UNESCO aims to give them a brief period of training before they go to their work. It tries to find teachers who are as close as possible in age to the group of adults they are going to instruct. And it tries to find teachers who will be sympathetic and patient and who will not "talk down" to their classes.

The reading material must be right, too. Adults are not going to find a real incentive to read if they are using books which were originally intended for children. There is a constant shortage of suitable reading material — and of writers!

Radio and television are being used all over the world today to teach people to read for the first time. Radio reading courses are in use in at least twenty countries and television techniques are rapidly being improved. Wherever possible students gather in groups so that common items of difficulty can be overcome and weak points in the broadcasts reported back to the authorities.

The consequences of becoming literate can sometimes be heart breaking. Many adults learn to read because they want to master new trade or a clerical job. They work hard and achieve literacy – only to discover that there is no suitable vacancy available or that further skills are required which they do not possess. Resentment and bitterness often result. It is obviously most important that the rewards which have been promised should be forthcoming.

Meantime UNESCO continues to co-ordinate, to plan, to conduct research and to experiment. Its Director-General has called the world-wide campaign against illiteracy "the most exalting venture of our generation".

1. Explore the possibility of showing one of the excellent films or film strips which UNESCO issues about illiteracy. (Your local UN representative may be able to help.)
2. You are planning a series of ten simple reading books for groups of middle-aged adults who have just learnt to read. Explain what subject matter you would include in the books and give reasons for the selection of it.
3. For further reading: *ABC of Literacy* by Mary Burnet (published by UNESCO 1965).
4. Discuss how different your lives would be if you could not read or write.

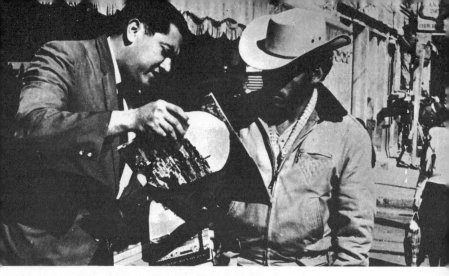

Selling magazine gospels in Mexico City

13   THE WORLD'S BEST SELLER

The Bible is big business in the world today. Parts of it have already been translated into nearly thirteen hundred different languages and dialects. Nearly one hundred million copies of Holy Scripture are issued each year. To many families in this country, whose one copy of the Bible is either mislaid or locked behind the glass doors of a bookcase, these facts may come as a surprise. This is partly because in Britain we can always obtain a Bible easily if we need one. Partly it is due to the fact that we have had the explosive material of the New Testament so long that it has ceased to shock us. Partly also it is because some of us (and most of our parents) were brought up on the King James version of the Bible — splendid, no doubt, for 1611, but written in language which is difficult for our 'swinging' society to understand.

In many other countries the situation is quite different. When something is in short supply, it makes you want to get hold of it. When a book is written in attractive, up to date language you want to read on. When perhaps only one gospel out of the whole Bible has been translated into your particular tongue, you want to find out what some of its other books have to say.

UNESCO is striving to make the world literate. If — perhaps we should say when — it succeeds, what will people read ? Will it be fiction—or classics—or biography? Or cartoon strips? Or the Bible?

53

Nobody can answer that question. If a man acquires the power to read, it is his right as an adult to choose his own material. Nobody should force him to read what he does not wish to.

The Bible Societies are aware of this. They know that cheap and trashy paper-back material is flooding the world. They also know that the Christian message, well translated and attractively produced, is as challenging and revolutionary as any in the world today. They know that it will always be up to date and relevant for the needs of men and women, and so they aim to produce and distribute Bibles whenever and wherever they are needed.

The British and Foreign Bible Society was founded in 1804 and it soon had agencies all over the world. Within twenty years other countries followed suit and soon there were Bible Societies in many European states and in America. For many years they worked independently of one another but latterly there has been close co-operation. Today the United Bible Societies of the world comprise over thirty member states which are responsible, between them, for Bible work in 120 countries of the world. Their experience, of course, varies considerably. Some of the members like the British and Foreign Bible Society, have been in existence over a century and a half whilst others are only a few years old. But they pool their financial resources in a World Budget and they plan their strategy together. In this way they are able to do what none of them could do singly. For instance, they can face up more realistically to the world population explosion and the growing numbers of literate people.

The Bible is, of course, in itself a library of sixty-six books, and the work of translating it into a completely new language is immense, time-consuming, and very costly. Binding, printing and distribution costs are also very high. Less than half of the cost of the scriptures circulated comes back to the Society by way of sales. The rest must be made up by voluntary contributions.

It is therefore common for "portions" and "selections" of scripture to be circulated. A portion is a complete book of the Bible, bound as a unit. The largest number of portions circulated are gospels, of which the favourite is St. John's. A selection is a unit less than a book, such as "The Sermon on the Mount" or "The Christmas Story". Not only is the circulation of portions and selections more economical, but many people believe they serve better as introductions to the Christian story than do complete Bibles, even where these exist.

Until a country is ready to form its own Bible Society most of the translation work must be done for it by societies like the British and Foreign Bible Society. As soon as possible, however, gifted nationals are brought in to share in the work and to prepare for the time when the country can free itself of its "missionary" apron-strings. It is interesting to note that ten national Bible Societies have been formed since 1961, several of them in "young" countries.

More Bibles are still printed in England than in any other country. A Bible is about ten times as long as an ordinary novel. In order to make it compact and not too heavy to handle it has to be printed on very thin paper. This means that to meet its demands each year the British and Foreign Bible Society uses about eleven thousand miles of paper, most of it no more than one thousandth of an inch thick ! On average it packs and ships one copy of the Bible every two seconds of every working day to different parts of the world. It prints the Bible, or parts of it, in nearly nine hundred languages or dialects and each year it uses more than 50,000 crates, cartons and postal packets in this vast operation.

A world-wide best-seller means big business !

———————◆———————

1. Further information about the British and Foreign Bible Society can be obtained from its Secretary for Schools and Colleges, 146, Queen Victoria Street, London, E.C.4.
   Other organisations, too, are working on Bible translation. Read *Two Thousand Tongues to Go* by Ethel A. Wallis and Mary A. Bennett, (Hodder & Stoughton), which describes the adventures of the Wycliffe Bible Translators throughout the world today, or write to them at Bletchingley Road, Merstham, Redhill, Surrey.

2. Using the Authorised (1611) Version of the Bible, look up the parable of the Good Samaritan (Luke Chapter 10). Try to re-write the story in simple, up to date English. Compare your result with others in your form, and with the way J. B. Phillips translates it.

3. Collect together as many translations of the New Testament in modern English as you can. Compare and contrast them. Which do you most enjoy reading? Why?

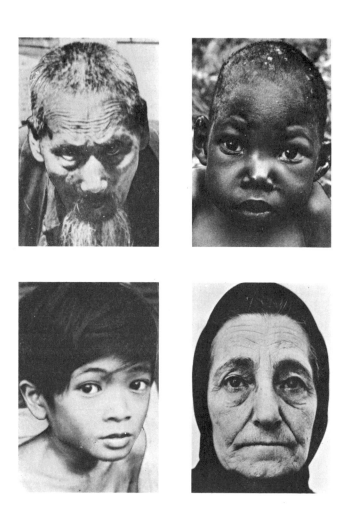

14   OXFAM

Oxfam, first known as the Oxford Committee for Famine Relief, was formed in 1942 by a group of people living in Oxford. It was set up in the first place to send prompt relief to the starving children of occupied Greece. With the passing years its work has gradually widened and today its objects can perhaps best be expressed by quoting from a leaflet put out by the organisation itself:

OXFAM

"Oxfam's main object is to relieve poverty, distress and suffering in any part of the world—whether due to a natural disaster, such as famine or earthquake; to war or civil disturbance, or to lack of resources among the people involved. It tries to achieve this object in many ways: by providing food, healing, clothing, shelter, training and education and by promoting research which in turn may help to relieve distress."

Though Oxfam continues to give priority to emergency help, the quotation indicates how the *prevention* of famine and hunger has gradually come to fill a larger role in the work. In a recent year, for example, only 4 per cent of aid was required for emergency relief. Just over 8 per cent was spent on actual feeding whereas 18 per cent of the money was spent on training, 20 per cent on medical work and 30 per cent on agricultural work. Obviously, in a bad year, with perhaps a whole series of natural disasters, these percentages might look very different. Meantime the positive, preventative side of the work continues.

The widespread backing which Oxfam now receives means that it can support a number of long-term projects designed to remove the causes of hunger and to raise living standards in various parts of the world. It may mean, for example, providing a peasant community with better seeds or better cattle over a period of several years. It may mean buying proper tools for them or improving their water supply. It may involve the provision of special vocational training courses to help refugees become self-supporting, or basic medical aid for a remote village. It may, in fact, take one of a hundred different forms in any one year.

Oxfam is non-sectarian and non-political. It sets out, therefore, to support organisations which are already working in a trouble-spot rather than establishing a complex field structure of its own. In this way, it believes, overlapping and waste of effort and personnel can be avoided.

An examination of Oxfam's grants for any given year seems to bear these facts out. Money is being allocated to Protestant, Roman Catholic and Greek Orthodox projects as well as to other smaller Christian groups. But it is worth noting also that grants have been given to Jewish and Muslim organisations as well as for work being done by non-religious groups. In fact, wherever a voluntary agency is fulfilling a real need, and is of proved integrity, Oxfam is willing to consider giving financial help.

The following examples picked out from among several hundred grants in one recent year illustrate the point :

The Salvation Army received a further £6,000 for its feeding programme in North and East Algeria : Quakers sponsoring a workshop for disabled refugees in Austria got £1,000 : the International Planned Parenthood Federation was granted £2,500 to provide a doctor, a nurse and essential propaganda material for work in Ceylon : in Brazil the Catholic Relief Services were given £3,000 to help families in Rio with new bedding following flooding: the Baptist Missionary Society received a grant for the fourth year in succession towards an agricultural training centre in Orissa, India. And so the list goes on !

Recently, with the great increase in the amount of aid available, Oxfam has appointed a small number of Field Directors of its own. Though each of them serves a very wide area, they are able to take an active part in organising some of the projects as well as discovering new areas of need. If they can find an organisation able and willing to meet that need, they can then arrange for the necessary financial help to be provided.

Many people, however, feel there are too many charities today. They become puzzled and sometimes angry when they receive appeal envelopes each year from several different organisations which appear to be doing the same sort of work. Oxfam claims to use its influence to promote co-operation between existing charities. It is exciting, therefore, to read that Christian Aid, War on Want and Oxfam are working jointly to provide a medical programme in the Messaad area of Algeria.

At present about ninety countries benefit from Oxfam's aid, and it is hoped that this number may increase still further. In this country a series of regional offices controlled by full-time professional organisers keeps the claims of Oxfam before the public. A whole army of volunteer helpers is also engaged in the work. The Headquarters in Oxford receives an average of about one thousand letters every day — and this becomes several thousand at peak periods.

Of every shilling given to Oxfam, 9¾d. is put to work overseas,

1$\frac{3}{4}$d. is used to raise more money and only $\frac{1}{2}$d. is spent on administrative costs. Oxfam's annual income is now approaching three
million pounds.

Some Oxfam supporters have become 'Pledged Gift' collectors,
recruiting their friends and neighbours as regular monthly sub-
scribers. They include an old lady of eighty and a boy of sixteen
who has more than one hundred members in his group. "Young
Oxfam" meetings are also becoming popular. These are groups of
young adults in the 15-25 age range who get together to learn more
about the world's needs and to help to raise funds. Links are also
maintained by Oxfam with schools, colleges and youth clubs, with
industry and with the Trade Unions.

Oxfam paints its canvas with a wide brush, yet much more still
remains to be done. The regional organisers, as well as the Oxford
Headquarters, can always find work for those with time to spare.

———◆———

1. Find out all you can about Oxfam's work. The booklet *Ways of
    Helping* may be useful.
2. "Some people quite inconsistently demand of a charity that it
    should both be efficient and spend nothing on administration . . . .
    Efficiency costs money . . . . To rely *entirely* on voluntary help, for
    example, invariably leads to inefficiency". (From Oxfam's *Notes
    for the Guidance of Voluntary Helpers*).
    Do you support this statement?
3. "This house contends that a solution of the problem of world
    hunger and its allied issues could more speedily be brought about
    if a merger of all the charitable organisations working in this
    field were effected."
    Debate this motion, and if possible invite a representative from
    one of the organisations concerned to speak to it.

15   SALLY TO THE RESCUE

Though the earliest attempts to train dogs for use by blind people were carried out in France nearly two hundred years ago, the first English trainer did not begin work until 1931. In October that year he completed the training of four blind persons and their guide dogs. From that small beginning, progress has been continuous. Today there are about 1,200 guide dog owners in Great Britain.

For many years now this valuable work has been carried on by the Guide Dogs for the Blind Association. The Association depends entirely on voluntary contributions, and funds are raised in many different ways. Schools play an important part in these efforts, particularly in the collection of silver paper and milk bottle tops.

When a blind person applies for a guide dog he is interviewed and his name is placed on a waiting list. The Association has four training centres and eventually he will be summoned to attend one of them for four weeks intensive preparation. During this important period, the dog meets its new owner and together they are helped to tackle every imaginable traffic situation and hazard. Guide dogs must be intelligent, willing and above all even-tempered. Labrador Retrievers are used mostly but some Alsatians, Golden Retrievers, Boxers and a few cross breeds are also trained.

The Association has a selective breeding scheme, but this by no means meets all its needs. In 1956, therefore, it introduced Puppy Walking. This enables the Association to put suitable puppies into private homes where they are taught to be obedient and also how to walk on the left-hand side of the handler and how to sit at the kerb. About half of these puppies later qualify as guide dogs. Their working life is about eight or nine years.

Though it costs about £250 to train a Guide Dog, a blind person is never asked to pay more than a token sum for his animal. The payment may be as little as five shillings, for it is the Association's policy that no applicant is ever refused a guide dog on financial grounds.

After a blind person leaves the training centre he is visited periodically to see that he and his dog are well and working correctly. If there are faults the trainer can probably correct them on the spot. If not, the dog and its owner may return to the centre for a few days in order to eliminate any shortcomings.

Dorothy Travers, who owns a handsome Yellow Labrador called Sally, was born blind. Her blindness was due to what is called "congenital cataract", but through the skill of surgeons she was able to obtain 'pinpoint sight' in her left eye. This meant she could only see what was directly in front of her and had to move her head about constantly in order to follow any moving object. Yet she was able to attend an ordinary school from the age of eleven, even though she always had to wear a pair of thick, ugly spectacles. Dorothy knew this partial sight would only last for a limited period. In fact she had it till she was thirty, and by that time she was happily married with three young children.

After she left school Dorothy had a varied career and tried several jobs. Whilst she was working as a secretary in London she met her husband and got married. Later they moved to the North of England, where Dorothy had been born. She was particularly proud of the fact that up to this time she had never used a white stick, and that most people did not know she was nearly blind.

When her sight finally gave out the shock to Dorothy Travers was greater than she had ever imagined it would be. She returned now to a sightless world, this time without any prospect of a temporary release from it. She became embittered and unhappy — and still she scorned a white stick, or any admission to the outside world that she was blind.

Then Dorothy's husband was taken seriously ill and she was compelled to seek registration as a Blind Person in order to apply for a job of work. A Home Teacher was assigned to her. After twelve months of gruelling training she qualified as a Braille Copyist. She has spent about twenty-six hours every week doing this work in her home ever since.

Before her training was completed Dorothy's Home Teacher persuaded her to apply for a guide dog. After some months of waiting she left home for Exeter and four weeks of training in handling a guide dog. There she met Sally, her Yellow Labrador, then twenty months old.

Dorothy and Sally have been inseparable companions ever since. Together they go out shopping, walking in the park, visiting friends — in fact they can go almost anywhere. Whether they are going across a busy zebra-crossing or simply taking a stroll, each knows exactly what the other wants to do by a series of signals.

Dorothy leads a normal life today — largely, she would say, because of Sally. She cares efficiently for her husband and three children and can cope with all the household chores herself. She

62

does all the washing and ironing as well as all the cooking and cleaning single-handed, and the Braille dials on her cooker and washer help make her an expert housewife.

But there is another important point. When she was younger Dorothy didn't have much time for religion, even though she attended Church and Sunday School as a girl. Yet now she takes a very active part in the life and work of her local parish church. She puts her change of heart down to Sally. 'You see', she told me when I went to talk with her, 'before Sally came I questioned everything — all the time — and what I couldn't get a clear answer to I refused to believe. And then it struck me that every time we went out together Sally was taking me round all sorts of obstacles and past all sorts of hazards which I knew nothing at all about — and I realised that I trusted her completely and had faith in her. And so it was that she taught me to have faith in God.'

Dorothy Travers works ceaselessly today on behalf of the Guide Dogs for the Blind Association. Whether talking to Church groups or to schools, to Scouts or to Guides, whether collecting tinfoil or raising money some other way, she can be seen out and about with Sally, her Yellow Labrador.

She wants to make certain that every needy blind person can have a dog like Sally to come to their rescue.

---

1. It may be possible to invite a person who was once able to see but is now blind, to talk to your form. Draw up a list of ten important questions you would ask your visitor.
2. The Guide Dogs for the Blind Association, 83/89 Uxbridge Road, Ealing, London, W.5. can supply pamphlets and further information, and will also advise you if there is a Guide Dog owner in your locality.
3. Read *The Story of my Life* by Helen Keller (Hodder & Stoughton Paperback 1966) and then prepare a short five minute talk on it.

16   VELLORE

Few hospitals in the world today are better known than the Christian Medical College and Hospital at Vellore, in South India — and probably none is supported by so wide a variety of people. In Britain today there is one doctor for about every 1,000 of the population, and one nurse for every 400. In the United States the figures are even better — one doctor for every 700, and one nurse for every 350. In India, one doctor must be shared by 5,000 people, and a nurse by 16,000! That is one reason why a large modern hospital like Vellore, with over 500 doctors and nurses, makes such a great impact in India today.

Vellore is a 1,000 bed hospital with a staff of 1,700. In addition to the 20,000 in-patients who are treated each year, thousands more receive treatment of one sort or another. Twice weekly, on Wednesdays and Fridays, a bus equipped with medical supplies goes on "Road Side" — and villagers within a radius of eighteen miles of Vellore attend the clinics which are set up under the trees. For those patients with eye troubles who cannot come to the hospital, "Eye Camps" are conducted every month in various villages. On an average about 50 operations are performed in each "Camp", a majority of them being for cataracts. In all, counting in-patients and out-patients, half a million people are treated by the staff of this great hospital every year.

Looking at the hospital today, with its modern facilities, its research centre and its training programmes for doctors and nurses, it is difficult to believe that it was all started by a fun-loving young woman at the turn of the century. Yet that is exactly what happened. Ida Scudder, staggered by the desperate shortage of doctors which she had seen in South India with her missionary parents, returned to the United States where she qualified as a doctor of medicine. In 1900 she went back to India, and with one untrained assistant to help her, set up her hospital — one bed on the verandah of her mother's home!

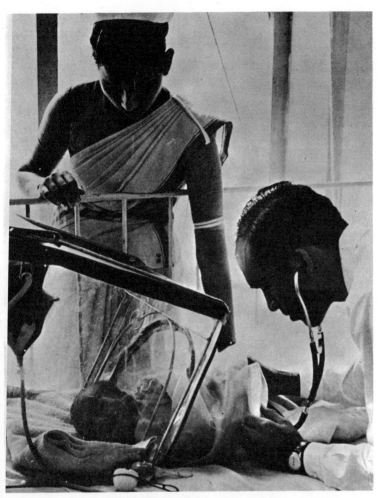

But Dr. Scudder's vision and determination won through. Within two years she had opened a hospital with 40 beds : by 1924 a 267 bed hospital had been built. And perhaps even more significant, a Nurses Training School was started in 1909, and a Medical College, which has already trained over 1,100 Indian doctors, in 1918. This courageous lady, who died at the great age of 90 in 1960, lived to see the work she had started acclaimed throughout the length and breadth of India as well as overseas.

Vellore is a place of many stories, and the life and work of Ida Scudder is one of the best of them. There are many more, but one must suffice for the purposes of this chapter.

Paul Brand, born in India and educated in England, had just finished his medical training and was ready to go back to India as a missionary doctor when in 1940 the bombs began to fall on London. Working in the casualty clearing stations, Dr. Brand soon found himself busy repairing arms and legs damaged in the air raids. In 1943, he varied his experience and began to specialise in treating polio cases. The war over, he went in 1946 to Vellore at the request of its Director, Dr. Cochrane, planning to remain only long enough to enable the hospital to obtain another surgeon. Then one day Dr. Cochrane took him to visit the leprosy sanatorium. There, as the patients came up to greet him, he saw many hands. But they were deformed, twisted hands. They were lepers' hands with stumps for fingers — paralysed, stiff and useless. Paul Brand stayed on in Vellore. Scores of doctors and surgeons, he knew, were working to heal polio victims. Yet the needs of the world's twelve million lepers were largely overlooked.

To begin with Dr. Brand spent months with a team of interested doctors, in research. They studied every book they could lay hands on which dealt with hand surgery. Then Paul Brand asked the Director to send him his first patient "with hands so bad they could not possibly be made worse". And he came, a young Hindu. Painstakingly Dr. Brand and his assistants operated on two fingers at a time, praying as they closed each wound. After many weeks of waiting it was obvious that the young patient was to have a useful pair of hands, and when he was finally discharged from Vellore there was new hope in his face as well as new strength in his fingers. Since that first operation Dr. Brand and his colleagues have repaired thousands of pairs of hands, as well as other limbs, and the "Brand Operation" has become known in medical circles all over the world.

Of course this is only one aspect of the wide and varied work which is carried on at Vellore. In a hundred other ways the doctors and nurses associated with this hospital are seeking to keep it bang up to date with modern surgical and medical progress and development.

Nor should it be forgotten that Vellore is a *Christian* Medical College and Hospital. Ida Scudder came to India as a Christian missionary, as well as a doctor, and today five full-time chaplains work amongst the patients and their families, helping them to understand something of the healing love of Jesus Christ. The chapels at both the Hospital and the College are central not only in situation but also in their significance. Prayers are offered before each operation takes place. At each Road Side clinic a hymn is sung, prayer is offered and a religious worker tells a bible story.

It is a tribute to all who work at Vellore that today more than forty Protestant denominations and missionary societies in ten different countries combine with the Church in India to support the hospital. Though of course most of the doctors and nurses are Indian, there are people on the staff from Great Britain, the U.S.A., Australia, Canada, Germany and the Netherlands. In Great Britain the hospital, as well as being supported by various missionary societies, is also helped by an organisation called Friends of Vellore. Each year a great musical concert is held in the Royal Albert Hall, London, at which the conductor and leading artists give their services free for the support of the College and Hospital. In this and other ways the work of Vellore, the greatest medical centre in all Asia, is carried forward.

1. Read *Dr. Ida* or *Ten Fingers for God* (both Hodder Paperbacks by Dorothy Clarke Wilson) for the full story of Dr. Scudder and Dr. Paul Brand.
2. Should a Christian missionary attempt to persuade a practising Moslem or Hindu to follow Jesus Christ?
3. Write to The Friends of Vellore, Vellore House, Claverly Villas, Finchley, London, N.3. for further information or to book speakers and visual aids.

17 THE CHESHIRE HOMES

Few names from the Second World War are better remembered in Great Britain today than that of Leonard Cheshire. The daring exploits of the young R.A.F. pilot officer who wrote *Bomber Pilot* and who was later promoted Group Captain and awarded Victoria Cross and a D.S.O. with three bars have often been talked about. The activities of 617 Squadron, which he commanded, were packed with drama and excitement.

Towards the end of the war Cheshire had a unique experience. He was sent for unexpectedly by Field Marshal Wilson, the head of the British Joint Staff Mission. Wilson told him that at their recent meeting in Potsdam the Allied leaders had decided to use atomic bombs against the Japanese. The British War Cabinet was insisting that as a matter of prestige Britain should be represented officially when the bombs were detonated by the Americans. Grudgingly, the American authorities agreed that one distinguished British scientist should fly in the raids, accompanied by one R.A.F. representative. Sir William Penney was the scientist. Group Captain Cheshire was the choice of the Royal Air Force.

An atomic bomb had already been dropped on Hiroshima. Cheshire and Penney were in an American bomber about forty miles away from the target when they saw the flash of the second atomic bomb over Nagasaki. It was followed by a billowing mushroom cloud which grew to mammoth proportions as they watched. Those who knew the effects of that flash realised that a new age had dawned for humanity. Man had manufactured a monster which might end up by destroying its maker.

To begin with Cheshire was both intrigued and fascinated by the power of the new atomic weapons. Many thousands of Allied lives, he knew, had been saved because the explosion of those bombs had forced Japan to surrender. Also, the Allies now had a powerful deterrent against war — a weapon so terrible that men would surely be too afraid to make war upon one another. It was only gradually that the horror and misery of what had happened at Nagasaki began to dawn upon him.

Soon after the Japanese surrender the war ended, and men and women began to return home from the forces. Some were badly disillusioned : nearly all of them very restless. Cheshire discovered that many of them, like himself, longed to find in peacetime the adventure and the comradeship they had known in the war. He became an unofficial spokesman and champion for unsettled ex-servicemen, devising several schemes to help them, but with little or no success. Leonard Cheshire began to wonder whether he would ever discover his true role in the difficult, post-war world. Meantime the nightmare of Nagasaki and the human suffering which followed it remained fresh in his mind.

It was his encounter with Arthur Dykes which proved a turning point in Cheshire's life. Dykes had worked with Cheshire in 1947. A cheerful little man, old before his time, he had gone into hospital where he was found to be suffering from cancer of the liver. Arthur Dykes had no known relatives or friends to turn to — yet because his complaint was incurable the hospital authorities did not want him ; they had a queue of curable patients waiting to occupy their few vacant beds. For days Cheshire pestered nursing homes, friends in the neighbourhood and charitable institutions, but all to no avail. Finally, he took Arthur Dykes in himself. He nursed him single-handed for three long, painful months until he died. Then he laid out the corpse and made all arrangements for the funeral.

About this time also Leonard Cheshire became a Roman Catholic. True, he had regarded himself as a Christian beforehand but recently he had begun to study religion with new interest and zest. He found peace of mind in his newly chosen faith.

As a result of all this, Cheshire decided to turn the house in which Arthur Dykes had died into a home for the chronic sick — and the story of the now famous Cheshire Homes really begins at that point. Since that first Home was opened in 1948 in Hampshire, over forty more have been started in the United Kingdom, with several more in course of preparation.

The Homes cater for people who are either permanently disabled or incurably sick — people like Arthur Dykes, for whom the hospitals can do nothing further. Because of this, they are run as homes and not as hospitals, and the aim of each Home is to provide an atmosphere of true affection and family life. The residents take

Creative activity in a Cheshire Home.

as much part as they are able in the day to day running of affairs. Each Home is managed by a local committee, and is privately owned, and therefore dependent on voluntary subscription. The Homes are undenominational, and no distinction is made on the grounds of a person's colour or social status. Patients are admitted simply according to their individual need.

When a new Home is being set up there is practically no kind of equipment that is not welcomed as a gift—clothes, linen, bandages, medicines — almost any household articles, as well as materials for the garden, are needed. And for those who can offer an hour or two's help each week in a Cheshire Home there is plenty of scope !

In 1955 Leonard Cheshire went with two or three helpers to India, hearing that there was a demand for Homes of a similar sort there. Though the little group had less than £100 between them when they landed, they bought an asbestos hut and began to take in a few patients. Soon great interest was aroused and support began to grow. Bigger, more permanent accommodation was built. By 1958 six Homes had been set up. Today there are nearly twenty throughout the length and breadth of India.

A similar story could be told for other countries, too. There are Cheshire Homes now in over twenty foreign lands — in Portugal and Papua, in Morocco and Malaysia. Sometimes they cater especially for mentally handicapped children, sometimes for leprosy cases, sometimes for people who are physically handicapped — and sometimes they are "general" Homes.

Thanks to the help and support of a great many people the world over, and the drive of Leonard Cheshire, the Homes have become the spearhead of a great movement for the relief of suffering.

1. A list of books, films and film strips covering the work of Leonard Cheshire and his wife Sue Ryder can be obtained from:
   The Secretary,
   The Mission for the Relief of Suffering,
   7 Market Mews,
   LONDON, W.1.

2. " ... to enable people to be made whole, their whole personalities must be served. The danger is to treat illness rather than a patient, to tackle problems rather than care for persons." Discuss these statements with reference to the work of:
   (a) the Cheshire Homes;
   (b) hospitals in Britain today.

3. There are about 656,000 people on the Disabled Persons' Register in this country. Many of them are employable. Find out what jobs they are doing in your area.

4. Discuss or debate these two early post-war statements by Leonard Cheshire:
   "The necessity of ending war is a biological necessity. It is a choice between survival and extinction." (November 1945)
   "Strength is once more measured in terms of guns, efficiency and dollars: the weak are still at the mercy of the strong, and we are already on the way towards another war." (April 1946)

18   A WORLD OF THEIR OWN

One of the greatest wonders of our modern age is the progress made by doctors and research workers in the battle against disease. Every year comes news of lives saved and men and women made happier because the illnesses from which they suffer have at last yielded to medical treatment.

Yet we know also that new diseases and viruses are appearing all the time, and it often seems that nature, having been defeated in one disease, sends along a new one to take its place.

It is quite possible that there have always been some autistic children but it is only very recently that autism, the disease from which they suffer, has been diagnosed. This childhood mental illness is very difficult to understand and even harder to treat. Though autistic children seem to be completely normal physically, they appear to live in a world of their own, withdrawn from all human contacts and relationships. Often they do not use speech; sometimes they may repeat a question which they have been asked in order to indicate their wishes ; at other times they merely echo what they have heard.

Only a very few years ago these children would have been rated ineducable and probably kept in a hospital for severely sub-normal children. Today, after research and experiment, the prospects for them seem altogether brighter. For example, there are several symptoms of the illness, and this helps doctors to diagnose it correctly and to distinguish it from other similar complaints. Also, several Centres for autistics have now been opened and there are plans for many more.

Moat Hall Autistic Centre near Eccles in Lancashire was the first of its kind in the North of England when it opened in June 1966. It occupies part of a former open-air school and the rest of the premises are now used by a youth club in the evenings. It has been skilfully equipped for the children's use. It is bright and colourfully decorated and it has its portable paddling pool and its climbing frames. The atmosphere is gay and happy.

The teacher in charge of the Centre had had wide experience of working with handicapped and maladjusted children before she came to Moat Hall. A member of the Society of Friends (or Quakers), she is happily married with two healthy children of her own. She makes no secret of the fact that her Christian faith plus her happy home life made her want to help severely subnormal children, and in particular those suffering from autism. All along she and the children she works with have received support and backing from the Education Authority and the local Education Officer.

Three boys and a girl, their ages ranging from five to nine were the first "pupils" at Moat Hall, and another girl of nine joined later. Each of them is brought every day to school by taxi. The three oldest children had earlier been judged ineducable, and to begin with only one had any speech.

It was obvious straight away that a very close link would have to be forged between the school and the parents. So it is that from the very beginning Moat Hall has been "at home" to any interested parents on one afternoon each week and that birthday parties are held with great pomp and ceremony at school as well as at home. There is a frequent exchange of news about the children, and mothers are able to help in some of the activities. Visitors too are given a warm welcome, though for the children's sake the number visiting the school at any one time must be kept low.

Watching them happily employed today, it is difficult to imagine that when these children first came to Moat Hall they either stood staring blankly into space or just simply walked about all day, perhaps crying, or laughing hysterically. The love and affection which have been shown to them at school as well as in their own homes is beginning to have its effect.

The teacher and her trained nursery helper set great store by the period of worship which is held soon after the children arrive at school each morning. With the children held safe in their arms, they tell them that they are going to be quite still — and for perhaps five minutes there is complete silence. The two adults know that at that particular time several other people in widely separated places are pausing briefly to pray for these five boys and girls.

Meantime, all the children are showing signs of progress, and in some cases it is very remarkable indeed. I watched as the children worked with various pieces of apparatus, some of it very expensive, some home-made. They sat contentedly together round a table, each absorbed in the task of the moment. Two of them were busy matching words to pictures, one was sorting out script letters — another was fitting together the pieces of a jig-saw puzzle. All of them can hold a crayon now and at least scribble with it, and each of them plays a percussion instrument and moves in some way to

music. Of course, there is no set time-table, but prayers, milk and
biscuits at eleven and a rest period after lunch help to break up the
day. When the sun shines and the weather is warm the children
love to play outside on the grass, in the sand pit or in the paddling
pool. There is much for them to do.

Because of the success which has so far been achieved another
'class' under a further teacher and helper has since been opened
there and new centres are projected for other areas. And all the
time, in this country and abroad, research goes on into the causes
and effects of autism, and into the best means of treating it. There
are courses and conferences which those interested in autistic
children can attend, and where all the latest information and
progress can be exchanged. At Moat Hall the teacher keeps a
detailed 'log' on each of her children, in which the special difficulties
of one child can be compared with those of another.

It cannot, of course, be claimed that the children at Moat Hall
are now being 'cured'. Until the causes of autism are known this is
perhaps too much to hope for. What *is* being shown, however, is
that in surroundings where affection and love are shown, children
can learn to work and play together — and in some cases achieve
much higher standards than was previously believed possible.

A visit to Moat Hall is a rewarding and satisfying experience.
Certainly for the teacher and her helpers there is as much
adventure and excitement as could be wished for.

1. Do you think a teacher who is a Christian can do a more effective
   job with mentally handicapped children than one who is not?
2. If you are interested in the effects of mental illness or handicap
   contact either:
   > The National Society for Mentally Handicapped Children,
   > 5 Bulstrode Street,
   > LONDON, W.1.

   or
   > The Society for Autistic Children,
   > 100 Wise Lane,
   > Mill Hill,
   > LONDON, N.W.7.
3. Some people say that mental illness and other kinds of handicap
   are the result of "original sin". Do you agree?

19 VOLUNTARY SERVICE OVERSEAS

In March 1958, with National Service in Britain over, a letter in the *Sunday Times* pointed to the large pool of gifted young men which had now become available. The writer was a churchman, Dr. Launcelot Fleming, then Bishop of Portsmouth. Dr. Fleming went on to point out that many of the Commonwealth countries had either just obtained or were on the road to independence, and he drew attention to the many appeals for volunteer assistance which they made.

Alec Dickson was at that time attached to the Education Department of the Nigerian Government. He was impressed by the challenge in Dr. Fleming's letter and followed up the ideas outlined in it. He worked hard through the summer of 1958 to recruit the first volunteers for service overseas. There were fourteen of them and all were boys. Ten went to Sarawak, two to Nigeria and two to Ghana. In the months that followed, VSO adopted its present name and appointed Mr. Dickson as its first Director. Valuable office space was loaned by the Royal Commonwealth Society and financial help was given by Christian Aid. Later still VSO was recognised as a Charity and is now governed by a Council through an Executive Committee.

From the first fourteen volunteers sent out in 1958, VSO had grown so that by 1962, 176 young people were sent to twenty-five countries. That 176 included apprentices from industry, some police cadets and a few graduates and more experienced volunteers.

On March 1st 1962 President Kennedy signed the Executive Order which inaugurated the American Peace Corps, thereby bringing great resources and government support to the aid of the United States' volunteer programme. This American initiative did much to help similar work in this country and soon it was announced that VSO had been chosen to run a pilot scheme to send thirty-six graduates to teach in West Africa. This scheme was named GVSO and this time the British Council helped with office space and administrative assistance.

A Volunteer tends a sick rhino in Tanzania.

Today VSO enlists young people under three main headings. The first one is the "Graduate and Qualified Teachers' Section", and as its name implies it recruits volunteers from Universities and Colleges and posts them to primary and secondary schools, teacher training colleges and sometimes Universities overseas. In 1966, 619 young men and women in this category went overseas on behalf of VSO.

The second type of recruit comes under the Development Section. 'Development' embraces a wide range of activities and includes agriculturalists, medical personnel, engineers, technicians, social workers and people from industry. Most of these volunteers are doing practical or research jobs, though a few of them are teaching and instructing in technical subjects. In 1966, 478 volunteers in this category went overseas.

The third section — Cadet Teachers' — usually recruits about 300 volunteers each year. Most of them come to VSO straight from school with one or more 'A' levels, and they go to teach in the junior forms of secondary schools overseas.

Training for VSO is a carefully planned affair. Attendance at a one-week briefing course prior to travelling overseas is compulsory for each recruit, and each course is geared to a particular country or area overseas. The aim is to provide a background knowledge of the country in question and to discuss some of the most common problems which are likely to be encountered, as well as to meet for the first time other volunteers going to the same area. VSO also arranges Skill Training Courses (such as Tropical Forestry and Tropical Medicine) where these are necessary, and Language Courses where a knowledge of the local language is felt to be essential in doing an effective job.

Recruits are usually flown out to their destinations in August or September, and VSO pays the return fare. The "projects" which the volunteers are going to help — whatever these may be — provide their keep and give them a spending allowance as well. Despite this contribution, the cost of running VSO is considerable. In 1966-67 nearly 1,500 volunteers were sent overseas, and this means that even with generous government help £160,000 had to be raised from a large number of private people and organisations to make the target programme possible. Often these contributors want to associate their financial support with a particular volunteer, and many young people find themselves sponsored in this way.

What sort of boys and girls enlist with VSO ? The story of Brian C. may help to answer that question. He was a Secondary Modern schoolboy who later trained as a fitter and turner, for which he had gained a City and Guilds Engineering Certificate. His hobbies included aero-modelling, outdoor athletics, motor-cycling and rugby.

When Brian went out to Addis Ababa in Ethiopia he found himself working alongside a doctor in an appliance workshop for ex-lepers. Brian made crutches but in his spare time he designed an artificial leg. He did this in the cheapest possible way by using rubber, gauze and plastic to produce a hard moulding. Needless to say, everyone was highly delighted with the results. A newspaper article said of Brian : "The thanks to B.C. are shown in the simple pathetic happiness on so many leper faces towards a young man from England who cared enough to come and give their lives meaning, a future and a possibility of dignity." The Secretary of the Fund for the Disabled in Addis Ababa wrote : "B.C. showed an example of volunteering and dedication to humanitarian activities of a very high order. He was ready to help in every way." Brian himself wrote, when he had come home, "I have returned a wiser, more experienced person ; it was a challenge."

The company for whom Brian works have taken him off the floor since his return and promoted him. They have since sent six more trade apprentices abroad through Voluntary Service Overseas.

Other volunteers cover a wide range of skills and professions. Michael B, a Technical schoolboy, went to help adapt an old Italian fort for use as a rehabilitation centre for cripples. Evelyn W., fresh from the Sixth Form of a girls' grammar school flew out to Pakistan to teach English and Music in a mission school. Bob S. was based at a mission hospital in Kenya and was able to re-organise the water supplies for the hospital, which included the building of a new dam.

There are many more fascinating case-histories which could be related if space allowed. Perhaps the comment of one V.S.O. volunteer after his spell of duty was over will serve to summarise the feelings of many others on their return to Britain. Asked what his advice was to the younger generation coming up behind him, he said "It's quite simple. If the chance comes to do something like VSO — take it ! "

1. Would you approve legislation making it compulsory for school-leavers to undertake six months voluntary service either at home or overseas? Give reasons for your decision.
2. Two useful addresses:
    (a) Voluntary Service Overseas,
         3 Hanover Street,
         LONDON, W.1.
    (who can put you in touch with a young person who has already been on V.S.O.).
    (b) Community Service Volunteers,
         Toynbee Hall,
         28 Commercial Street,
         LONDON, E.1.
    (C.S.V. was founded in 1962 to help young people to gain first-hand experience of social problems by undertaking projects in Approved Schools, Children's Homes, Hospitals and so on: but their work covers a wide range of other activities also.)
3. "Britain cannot afford to support schemes like V.S.O. She should first make sure her own economy is sound before helping other nations to strengthen theirs."
    Debate or discuss this statement.

When the Second World War ended Joyce Pearce was teaching History to sixth formers in a London girls' school. She encouraged her pupils to study current affairs and problems as much as possible, but she was surprised to discover how disillusioned they were about the future. Many of them seemed, in those difficult post-war days, to have lost all faith in any real purpose or reason for living. Miss Pearce therefore started an after-school discussion group, and this proved very popular from the start. But there was not sufficient time to deal with matters thoroughly, and often it was obvious that expert speakers were needed to discuss questions about religion, politics or world affairs in real depth.

Joyce Pearce talked the problem over with two of her colleagues, Ruth Hicks and Margaret Dixon. It seemed that a "base" where weekend residential courses could be held might meet the need. This would enable sixth formers from other schools — boys as well as girls — to attend. "Ockenden" in Woking, a late-Victorian family house with a large, wooded and untidy garden was made available by Miss Pearce's mother. Voluntary work-parties of sixth formers spent that summer helping to paint and re-decorate the house : camp beds and blankets were bought from ex-Army surplus stock : second-hand furniture was donated for living-rooms, and the first "Conference" was held in the Spring of 1948.

In May 1951 Kenneth Hyde, a Nonconformist minister and Youth Organiser arranged a weekend conference on Film Appreciation, and he showed a documentary about the plight of young people in the Displaced Persons' camps of Europe. A long discussion followed, and it became obvious that these sixth formers really wanted to *do* something to help solve this problem. From that moment the Ockenden Venture was born, and ever since it has been planning and working on behalf of refugee children.

From the very beginning the Venture has been concerned especially with the education of the refugee children it has been helping. Of course this does not mean that it has not cared about

The Original Five Ockenden Girls.

their physical well-being. Nor does it mean that young refugees have ever been brought to England solely because they seem to be more intelligent than the others. It *does* mean that Ockenden is the only voluntary refugee organisation in Europe which is providing specifically educational opportunities for refugee boys and girls so that they can earn their living and stand on their own feet in the country of their choice.

The Venture really began in the Spring of 1952 when two Polish and three Latvian girls came to live at Ockenden. Largely because of the wonderful progress of these first five girls (one gained nine G.C.E. 'O' levels in two years), the Ockenden Venture was recognised as a registered Charity in 1955. Since then over 800 children and young people have lived and studied under the scheme. There are now sixteen Ockenden houses in different parts of England and Wales, as well as a Home and four schools for Tibetan children in India. Boys as well as girls have been included in the Venture since 1956.

Ockenden's family is an international one. In the first years mainly German refugee children were helped, but since then Ockenden's young people have been Czechoslovakians, Estonians, Hungarians, Latvians, Lithuanians, Yugoslavs, Poles, Rumanians and Ukrainians and more recently Tibetans and Africans.

Once they have learnt English, the children who come to Britain go out to local schools. Some (including two of the first five) have already graduated from University or College, some are now working for University entrance, many are serving apprenticeships in Engineering, Draughtmanship, Catering and Horticulture. Others are nursing or working in offices, and there is even a zoo-keeper, a trainee locksmith, a jewel setter, and three boys at sea. Some of the young people return home to find jobs, a few have emigrated to Canada or the U.S.A., but many remain in this country.

It is Ockenden's policy to ensure that the children keep in close touch with their parents, and every boy or girl for whom it is possible is reunited with their family for seven or eight weeks during the long summer holiday. Many of the Ockenden staff also visit the parents at this time of year, and so the family links are maintained.

In the last few years the Ockenden Venture Family Trust has enabled older relatives to come to Britain, and now nearly 100 refugee children are living with their own family in various parts of England as a result of the Trust's work.

Today the number of refugee children in Europe needing the Venture's help is fast diminishing. This is because, as a result of World Refugee Year in 1959-60, the camps in Germany are nearly all closed and the former inhabitants have either emigrated or been re-housed in nearby blocks of flats. In 1963, however, a request came for help with Tibetan refugees. Through its Volunteer programme Ockenden has started two kindergartens, one secondary school and one vocational training school in India for Tibetan children This is in addition to financing an Art School at Mussoorie in the foothills of the Himalayas, where some of the 1,200 Tibetan children concentrated there are learning the traditional forms of art.

At Messaad on the edge of the Sahara in Southern Algeria, Ockenden is starting a pioneer school for young girls of Arab families. Oxfam has provided the funds and a young Ockenden volunteer-architect has designed the building and supervised its construction. Two teachers, one British and one Algerian, will run classes to teach up to thirty young girls the basic elements of house-craft, hygiene, first-aid and baby welfare. When these girls eventually go into "purdah", Ockenden hopes they will be able to introduce a higher standard into their home life, which in turn will react on the health and wellbeing of the whole community in which they settle.

Owing to political upheavals in Africa during recent years thousands of refugees have been on the move there. During 1966 and 1967 Ockenden received twelve African students into its houses in England. All of them had the ability, but no opportunity, to obtain University education in their country of origin. Of this group, the first two are now going on to universities in this country.

Owing to the Middle East War in 1967 thousands of Arab children faced a desperate situation. Along with other members of the International Council of Voluntary Agencies, Ockenden was asked to assist and did so at once. At any time members of the staff may be called upon to visit a new trouble spot somewhere in the world in order to decide what help the Venture may give. As far as resources and funds allow, that help will always be willingly and immediately given.

———◆———

1. Sets of mounted colour transparencies showing all aspects of the work of the Venture are available from:
   > The Ockenden Venture,
   > White Rose Lane,
   > WOKING,
   > Surrey.

2. Do you think it is important for a refugee organisation to lay special emphasis (as Ockenden does) on education? If so, why?

3. Imagine you are working as a teacher with a small group of refugees of secondary school age in a transit camp. They have received no previous education, and your time with them is very limited. What would you put into a course of ten Religious Education lessons? Would you modify your course (and if so, how), if you later discovered that the children's parents, with whom they later hoped to be re-united, were members of a different faith?

21   THE MAYFLOWER FAMILY CENTRE

"The Mayflower is a large mock-Tudor building" the travelling instructions said. "The front door is in Cooper Street under a blue board." We had travelled from Westminster Bridge and through the City of London, keeping the River Thames on our right all the time. We had come along East India Dock Road passing signs for Stepney, Poplar and Bethnal Green on the way. And now we had reached Canning Town, another part of London's vast dockland area, and found the Mayflower Family Centre.

From the roof of the building everything around us spelt activity. We saw the cranes in the docks, the huge cooling towers, and new blocks of flats and maisonettes mixing in with streets of tiny, terraced houses. Close by was the market with its jellied eels — and here and there an open space, still derelict. And here in the middle of it all, the Mayflower Family Centre.

Inside the Centre there was much to see and much to learn, but first of all a welcome from the Warden, Rev. David Sheppard. Most cricket enthusiasts know something of his story. The young man who captained the Cambridge University First XI in 1952 also became a Christian whilst he was a student there. His career as a member of the Sussex team and as a Test cricketer made him a popular hero with many teenagers. But before his cricketing career was over David Sheppard had become a Church of England minister and in 1957 he was appointed Warden of the "Mayflower", as it is known to the people of Canning Town.

Before he had been long at the Centre Mr. Sheppard discovered that when young people in the area fell in love and got married they usually wanted to move out to a suburban district to set up their home. He found out, too, that most of the leaders and workers in Churches and youth clubs of the area were people who travelled in on Sundays or on a weeknight. It looked as though it might be difficult to find leaders for the Mayflower from the locality. If they were to work effectively as Christians in Canning Town, Mr. and

Discussion group at the Mayflower.

Mrs. Sheppard realised that they must be prepared to live in the area for a long time and, as David Sheppard puts it, "to offer long-term friendship." Since they moved into their flat in the Mayflower in January 1958 they have been doing just that.

Working alongside the Warden and his wife there is a full-time staff of nine. This includes the Headmistress of the Nursery School which is housed within the Centre. It includes the Youth Leader and his Deputy, the Housekeeper and so on. Each of the staff has a particular group of jobs to do. In addition, the Centre contains a Hostel which can accommodate thirty people. Usually it is full, mostly with young men and women who have full-time jobs during the day. Some of them stay only a few weeks, some remain a year or two — but they come to offer what leisure-time help they can to the staff in running the Centre. After a spell at the Mayflower many of them feel more certain about the sort of job they want to take up when they leave. Some of these people have become ministers, some have gone into teaching and several have become social workers.

As its full title implies the Mayflower is much more than just a youth centre. It caters quite literally, from its Nursery School through to its Grandfathers' Club, for men and women from the cradle to the grave. But it would only be fair to admit that it is probably its youth work which has made the Mayflower so widely known in London. Most of the usual youth club facilities are provided and the Centre is particularly fortunate to possess a good swimming bath.

Some young people, however, come just to talk. Sometimes these discussions have taken place in the youth leader's flat, sometimes in the club rooms. Often they have gone on until a late hour. But through them many young people have come to accept Jesus Christ as the guide for their lives, and many who have not reached that stage have at least been able to resolve some of their deepest problems and to ask as many questions as they dare.

The Warden and the staff know that if real Christian work is to be done in Canning Town it is essential that there should be young people willing, when they get married, to settle down in the area and not move away. One of the first aims of the Centre is to build up a *local* Church of *local* families. Already there are several young couples who are helping to do this by settling in the area after their marriage and by continuing to help in the work of the Mayflower. This solid nucleus of young people is providing the local leadership which the Centre needs. It is also a powerful aid to David Sheppard and his staff.

Because it is so much like a very big family, the Centre finds itself helping its young members — and its older ones too — with a host of questions and problems. Sex and marriage, difficulties at work, money — all these subjects, as we shall see later in this book, are discussed freely and frankly.

But the work of the Mayflower does not end when the discussions are over. Prayer plays an important part in the life of the Centre and each day the staff have a list of those with special problems, for whom they wish to pray individually. It is no surprise, therefore, to find that the Mayflower's Church plays a large part in the life of this community in London's Dockland. When David Sheppard first went to Canning Town the church building was unheatable and so for seven years one of the club-rooms was used as a chapel instead. Through the efforts of the teenagers, working with some of the older members of the congregation, the large Church is now in use again. The building has been re-decorated and most of the old chocolate-brown paint has gone. A new heating system has been installed. It is here that many of the Mayflower young people have been married ; this is the church to which they have often brought their babies for baptism.

The Mayflower story is not yet complete. In David Sheppard's words : "The numbers who come to our church and our clubs and groups cannot be a safe guide. Only after many years will it be possible to see if a strong Christian work has been planted with its roots firmly embedded in local leadership."

Meantime, that work goes on.

1. "When Jenny was born, several neighbours said to Grace, 'You won't bring her up here, will you?' " (David Sheppard).
   Do you think the Sheppards are doing the right thing in bringing up their daughter in Canning Town?
2. " . . . to hammer the discipline of daily reading of the Bible at those who have not been in the habit of reading for pleasure can have . . . very bad effects." (David Sheppard)
   Discuss this statement, and suggest what some of the bad effects might be.
3. For further reading: *Parson's Pitch* by David Sheppard (Hodder & Stoughton, 1964).
4. In 1969 David Sheppard was appointed Bishop of Woolwich. Follow his career and find out all you can about a Bishop's work and responsibilities.

Oberammergau, a prosperous little town of smart hotels and wood-carvers' shops nestles close into the lovely woods and mountains of Bavaria. In summer-time it is busy and crowded with busloads of tourists and with pilgrims who come from far and wide to see the place which has become world-famous for its Passion Plays.

No one knows exactly when the first passion play was performed in Oberammergau, but 1633 is a date which every child in the village knows off by heart. In that year Oberammergau was afflicted with a severe outbreak of the plague, not unlike the one which broke out in London thirty-two years later. Some eighty-four people died of it, and so the village councillors conferred together and made a solemn vow. If the plague would subside, they would present from then onwards, every ten years, a play telling the story of the last week in the life of Jesus Christ. Legend has it that no further outbreaks of the plague ever occurred in Oberammergau after this resolution was made.

The play was put on in 1634 and every ten years up to 1674. In that year it was decided to advance the date for the next play to 1680. Since that time, except for the years 1920 and 1940, which were affected by the wars, the play has been faithfully performed every decade. In the earliest years, the play was given in the Parish Church, and only one performance took place. On the last occasion, in 1960, ninety showings were staged in a vast theatre and more than half a million spectators saw the play.

There are many features of the Oberammergau Passion Plays, however, which make them unique. For example, all those who take part must either have been born in Oberammergau itself or have resided there for at least twenty years. In 1960, about 1,400 people collaborated in the production of the Passion Play. Of these, about 800 were actors and there were 125 speaking parts. In addition, there was a choir of fifty and an orchestra of sixty. The remaining participants were busy as stage hands, ushers, wardrobe assistants and so on. Since the population of Oberammergau is only about 4,500, the involvement of 1,400 citizens in the play places a considerable burden on the town.

Christ before Pilate — a scene from the 1960 Production.

Preparations for the play begin nearly two years before it is staged. After a formal resolution to present the play has been passed by the village council, a special Passion Play Committee is appointed, which in turn delegates the detailed planning to a number of sub-committees. According to ancient tradition everyone who is entitled, by birth or residence, to take part in the play receives

The Theatre and Choir at Oberammergau.

an invitation, one year before it is presented, to allow their hair to grow long. Next, a casting committee ascertains the talent and ability of individual actors by means of public auditions and trials. Then, seven clear months before staging, the actual casting takes place — amid considerable publicity and a great deal of local suspense. In choosing actors for the various roles, the committee takes into account not only the talent and the appearance of the various actors, but also their suitability from the point of view of character. On selection day the whole village assembles in Church for a solemn service. Thereafter, rehearsals are held every weekday throughout the autumn and winter for the next seven months.

Because the importance and fame of the Passion Plays has increased steadily over the years, a very high individual standard of performance is demanded. In order to train promising actors "Exercise Plays" are presented in a small theatre in the village every year during the nine years between each performance of the

Passion Play proper. Sometimes these productions are classical plays, sometimes they are based on biblical subjects. In this way rehearsals for the next Passion Play are really going on all the time, for only the very highest standards are acceptable to the committee.

The performances are held in a magnificent theatre with a seating capacity of over 5,000. Long tiers of seats descend in a gentle slope towards the stage. Around and above the stage can be seen the hills and the blue sky, and though there is provision for the orchestra and scenery to be protected from rain, the actors themselves are always in the open air, regardless of weather conditions.

Each performance of the play occupies a whole day. It begins at 8.30 in the morning and goes on till six o'clock in the evening, with a break of two hours for lunch. These performances begin in May and continue, four or five times each week, until the middle of September.

The actors, of course, have various occupations. Of those who took parts as Christ's disciples in the 1960 productions, several are woodcarvers, two are farmers and one is a dairyman. Anton Preisinger, who played the part of Jesus in both 1950 and 1960, is the proprietor of a busy hotel in Oberammergau. A tall, striking, athletic figure, he talked frankly about his role. He spoke about the physical strain of the performances, which involve carrying a wooden cross weighing 80 lbs., and then being suspended from it for twenty-eight minutes every time the play is given. But he spoke also of the tremendous privilege which he had felt in being able to take part in two successive productions of the Passion Play, which sets its imprint not only on those who take part, but on the many thousands who come, every ten years, to watch and to listen.

---

1. "The presentation of a Passion Play would be ten times more effective if it took place in present-day dress." Discuss this statement.

2. "It is wrong to portray the person of Jesus Christ in plays, films or on television." Debate this statement.

3. Do you consider that a wider use of drama in church services would make the gospel message easier to understand? List as many points "for" and "against" as you can, and give reasons for each.

23   ANCIENT AND MODERN

Millions of people in the world today enjoy music of one sort or another, and it has been so for as long as man can remember. Music has also been used a great deal for religious purposes, and no-one can possibly estimate the importance of the part it has played in the story of Christianity. In Old Testament times Jewish worshippers came up regularly to the Temple in Jerusalem for great musical festivals. The early Christians sang psalms, hymns and spiritual songs and few services today would seem complete without singing.

One annual event which proudly traces its history back to the early years of the eighteenth century is the Three Choirs Festival, which claims to be the oldest musical festival in existence. The "Three Choirs" are those of the Anglican cathedrals of Hereford, Gloucester and Worcester, which are less than thirty miles apart from one another and lie in a triangle in the south-west of England. We shall perhaps never know now just how it was that the three choirs decided to meet together every year at one of the three cathedrals in turn. We do know, however, that in July 1713 there was a "general thanksgiving" in Worcester Cathedral following the signing of the Treaty of Utrecht, and that an orchestra as well as singers was provided in the cathedral for this event. It may well be that Worcester had invited the choirs from Gloucester and Hereford to join in these celebrations and perhaps the choirs then decided to meet together in another of the cathedrals the following year. At any rate, a three-yearly cycle seems to have been established before 1720 and it has continued (except for interruptions like the two World Wars) ever since.

The first "music meetings" (the word "festival" was not used until the early 1900's) lasted for only two days. Each morning the combined choirs sang morning service together in the cathedral, accompanied by the organ and an orchestra, and in the evenings a secular concert was held somewhere in the town. They were gay, carefree occasions, these early festivals. When the evening concert was over there were parties and dances, and sometimes they lasted till four o'clock the following morning! But since the singers were unlikely to meet their friends from the other choirs for another twelve months it was understandable that they wanted to make the very most of their time together.

Quite early on, however, it became clear that they wanted to do more than just meet together to enjoy themselves. In 1724, at Gloucester, it was suggested that a collection should be made at the cathedral door. That first offering realised £31 10s. 0d. and it was used to help and educate the orphans of members of the three choirs or of clergymen who had served in the dioceses of Gloucester, Hereford or Worcester. More recently these annual collections, which are still used for similar purposes, have sometimes exceeded £3,000.

After the early years the festivals became longer. The standard of the music sung and played was very high and the most famous musicians and singers in the world performed at the concerts, nearly all of which were now held in the cathedral. In 1878 Edward Elgar played the violin in the Festival orchestra with his father and in 1902 he appeared again, this time to conduct the second ever performance of his immortal work "The Dream of Gerontius". The festivals became famous, and visitors began to travel from all parts of the country and, eventually, from abroad. New works as well as old-established favourites were introduced and several composers over the years have written music with the Three Choirs in mind.

The high standards set in days gone by have been maintained. Today, the Three Choirs Festival is as securely established in the musical life of this country as ever. And despite the changes which passing years have brought it remains essentially what it was in its inception —a happy, as well as a great, religious and musical occasion.

Music of a very different kind was made by The Joystrings, the Salvation Army pop group which gave its last public performance in July 1968. The Joystrings' story, like that of many another group, is an interesting one, and it began in a curious way. Joy Webb, Peter Dalziel and Bill Davidson were all in training as Salvation Army officers when, in 1963, the Army appointed a new general —

Three of the Joystrings stirring a Christmas Pudding.

Frederick Coutts — to lead its work. Joy, Peter and Bill had each taken a second-hand guitar with them when they went to London for training but they were still very much amateurs in their skill with that instrument. Little did they realise how quickly they would have to become expert in its use !

In his first press interview General Coutts stressed the need for the Army to keep in touch with the people : to talk their language and to go where they are. "You mean going into coffee-bars ? "

94

asked a young reporter. "If the people are there, of course ! " said the General. "To use coffee-bar music ? " someone else asked. "Why not ? " came the reply. "That's our tradition — we employ the language and the music of the people."

Almost immediately the Army's International Training College in London was besieged with enquiries for the new Salvation Army "sound". It was not yet born, however ! Quickly the Training Principal called his students together. "We'll form an official rhythm group," he said. "Captain Joy Webb, you'll take charge."

Auditions were held among those at the College with guitars but after a trial period the guitar strength of the group was cut and Joy, Bill and Peter became the three remaining instrumentalists. They needed a first-class drummer and before long they found one in Wycliffe Noble. "Wyc", like the other three, was the son of Salvation Army officer parents. An architect by profession, he had received professional training as a boy in modern tone drumming and was an expert percussionist. Because he owned his own business, "Wyc" was able to give his services to the group. The other members received the same frugal allowance as other Army officers of equivalent rank. All the group's income went to Salvation Army funds, and the Army bore the costs of instruments, equipment and so on.

It did not take the Joystrings long to discover that, as one of them put it, "the pop business is ninety per cent hidden hard slog, and ten per cent stage work." Yet they were considerably helped by Joy's discovery that she could write original songs in the new style. Subsequently, Bill and Peter also discovered that they, too, had this gift. And at a time when the group badly needed a new sound, Nigel Robson, a young Salvationist from Stockport joined the group.

As their technique improved, so invitations to appear up and down the country began to come in. There was the exciting experience of making their first recording and later finding themselves "in the charts". There were the exhausting personal appearances, with the audience screaming for more. There were lightning tours with many miles of travelling—and television, bringing them within the sight and sound of millions of ordinary people. And all the time, for them, there was the constant reminder that they were "in business" not primarily for their own benefit but to proclaim a message, and preach the gospel in song.

Nearly always when the Joystrings visited a town or city for an evening appearance there were enquiries from those who, as a result of what had been sung or said, wanted to know more about the Christian faith. So it was arranged that there were always experienced Christians present in the audience to act as counsellors and advisors when the evening was over.

Invitations to appear abroad came in too. On one occasion the Joystrings spent a few days in France doing a programme which ranged from an appearance at a famous night club to playing on the barge on the River Seine where homeless men are cared for every night by the Salvation Army. Other overseas tours were soon planned and the problem of learning to sing in many foreign languages became a serious one!

Wycliffe on the drums, Joy singing and playing organ, and Bill, Peter and Nigel on vocal and guitars. That was the Joystrings. And somehow, despite the rush and bustle and tension, they managed to keep their heads.

For them, all the time, it was Pop with a Purpose.

1. It has been suggested that much of the ritual and music used in cathedral worship today is two hundred years behind the times. Do you agree with this statement or not?
2. Was William Booth right in his contention that there is no such thing as 'secular' music?
3. How would you meet the objections of those who maintain that it is wrong for a Christian group to sing in a nightclub?
4. For further reading: *Joy and the Joystrings* by A. J. Gilliard (Lutterworth Press, 1967).
5. Much of the world's greatest music is religious. Study the life of one great composer of such music. Prepare a short talk about him which can be illustrated by records.

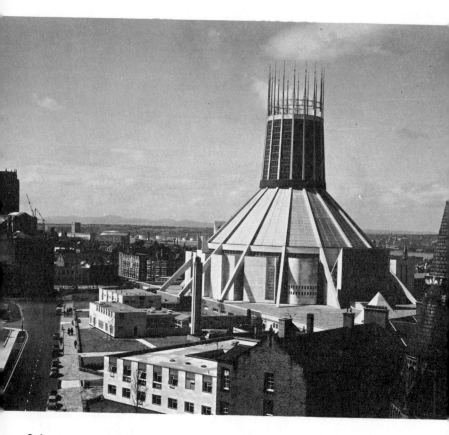

24   CITY OF TWO CROWNS

For a long time Liverpool has been world-famous as one of Great
Britain's leading cities and seaports. In recent years it has become
renowned as the centre of the "Mersey Sound" — the music which
young people the world over have found fascinating and compelling.
Today Liverpool is famous for another reason. Two fine modern
cathedrals — one Protestant and one Roman Catholic — now grace
its skyline.

Liverpool today is a busy, friendly place, but it has not always
been so. One of the unhappiest features of the city's history was the
hatred which existed for many years between Roman Catholics and

Protestants. In days gone by bitterness was intense and often physical violence was done by one section to the other. A few traces of that ill-feeling still linger on, but on the whole the relationship between the two denominations in the city is a great deal happier today. This is due in no small measure to the fact that Christians of all kinds are at last beginning to realise that the things they agree about are far more important than the things which still separate them.

Yet though there was often bitterness between one denomination and the other in bygone days, it did not stop Christian people from dreaming their dreams. The Roman Catholics of Liverpool, for instance, have been planning and praying for their new cathedral for well over a century. Many of them were poor, but their hearts yearned to build a great Church to the glory of God. It would be beautiful, as so much in their lives was not. It would be a monument in glass and stone to their simple faith. It would express the longings and aspirations of their hearts.

The long waiting of 114 years is now a memory. Consecrated and opened as recently as May, 1967, the Roman Catholic Cathedral of Christ the King was constructed in less than five years — more quickly than any other cathedral in the world. Yet, by contrast, no other cathedral scheme in modern times had taken longer to come to fruition.

Several designs had been accepted over the years but delays and rising costs had caused each of them to be eventually abandoned. In 1959, aware of the keen disappointment and frustration of their people, the Roman Catholic authorities decided to invite architects to submit designs for a new cathedral, and a competition was opened. In all, 298 entries were received from architects all over the world. The successful design was that of an English architect, Mr. Frederick Gibberd. It is undoubtedly a most exciting one.

The Archbishop of Liverpool and his advisers had asked for a cathedral whose main worshipping space would hold between two and three thousand people, so arranged that all of them could see the altar, but with none of them sitting much more than about seventy feet from it. To meet this requirement the plan is a central one — and from a distance the building looks rather like a vast tent surmounted at the top by a mighty crown.

As you enter the cathedral your eyes travel around the great circular shape and upwards to the lantern tower with its multi-coloured glass, which gives a wonderful sense of light and space to the inside of the building. Immediately below the tower, at ground level, is the altar, a rectangular block of white marble, and above it a huge canopy hangs suspended from the roof. Around the perimeter of the building are ten chapels, two of them larger than the rest, but each quite different from the others. Beneath the church there is a lower floor containing a large car park from which a lift and a stairway lead above. The outside colour scheme is grey and white and the cathedral is 290 feet high, topped off with sixteen pinnacles symbolising the Crown of Thorns — truly a kingly emblem for this modern, bustling city.

The Protestants of Liverpool also had their hopes and their ambitions. The new diocese of Liverpool had been carved out of the ancient diocese of Chester in 1880 because of the rapid growth of population and of industry. It had its Bishop, but as yet no cathedral. By the turn of the century, however, an Appeal Fund had been opened and an architect found, also as the result of a competition.

Giles Gilbert Scott was only twenty-two years old when his first drawings were submitted, and the construction of the cathedral was carried out under his personal supervision for more than fifty years. Had it not been for two world wars he would almost certainly have seen his great plan completed. A magnificent site was acquired for the new building and the foundation stone was laid by King Edward VII in 1904. The cathedral was consecrated in 1924 in the presence of King George V and Queen Mary. It was the first cathedral to be built in the North of England since the Reformation.

At an early stage in the planning Scott modified his design drastically. Instead of the twin towers originally planned he sub-stituted one great central tower, crowned with pinnacles of stone. Few people who compare the original scheme with the present design can doubt the wisdom of what Scott did. The cathedral is a vast, regal building raised in sandstone quarried from a site only five miles away. It is in the Gothic style of architecture and has been called "one of the noblest churches in Christendom". Built on a tremendous scale, nearly one quarter of it remains unfinished.

Continually rising costs, two world wars and bomb damage have made progress much slower than was originally hoped. Nobody knows exactly when the work will be finished. Meantime the worship of ministers and people goes on alongside the hammering of masons and craftsmen. There is a fine tradition of music at the cathedral and the organ, with its nine thousand pipes is reported to be the greatest instrument of its kind in the world.

Since Liverpool had its two cathedrals it has often been remarked that the architect of the Anglican cathedral was a Roman Catholic and that the architect of the Roman Catholic is a Protestant. Some people see something symbolic in the fact that the road which links the two great churches is called Hope Street, and look forward to the day when all the Christian churches are united. Meanwhile, the crowns of the two cathedrals point upwards to the sky — a reminder not only of the arguments and disagreements of men, but also of their hopes and aspirations.

———————————

1. Read St. Mark Chapter 14 vv.3-9, preferably in a modern translation. To what extent do you feel this passage answers the objections of those who claim that a new Cathedral is out of place in a hungry world?

2. Would Christianity be a greater force in the world today if worshippers met in small groups in one another's homes? Find out all you can about early Christian worship before you write down your answer.

3. Either:
   Make a list of *all* the cathedrals in this country, finding out when each was built, and in which particular style of architecture,
   or:
   Visit *one* cathedral and make a small booklet about it, illustrating it if possible with photographs.

Shelter gave new hope as well as a new home to this family.

25   WORKING FOR SHELTER

Millions of men and women watching B.B.C. television one night
in 1967 got a severe shock. A play, written by a young man called
Jeremy Sandford was screened during the peak viewing hour. The
title of the play was 'Cathy Come Home'. It won a television award.
What's more, it made such an impact upon those who saw it that
the B.B.C. decided to show it again some weeks later. The play
sketched the life of a newly married English couple with a young

family — and showed the bitter struggles they had to secure a decent place to live. The thing that staggered the viewing public was that every incident depicted in the play was based on fact. And even though this was made clear, some people still refused to believe that such a story could possibly be true of Britain in the sixties.

Here are some facts about housing in our country today :

1. The Ministry of Social Security stated that in 1967 1,420,000 children in this country were living in overcrowded conditions.

2. The Annual Report of the Ministry of Health for 1966 states : "Of the 12,411 people in hostels for the homeless on one night last year 8,160 — just under two-thirds — were children."

3. In London, nearly one house in every five is, at the time of writing, multi-occupied — and 150,000 families are on council waiting lists !

4. In Glasgow you can find 25 of Britain's 40 most overcrowded districts — and 120,000 families have no bath. More than a fifth of the families in that vast Scottish city share the w.c. with other households.

5. In Birmingham, our second largest city, more than 500 families find themselves on the streets and are taken into temporary hostels every year.

6. In Liverpool, 70,000 occupied houses have been designated "unfit for human habitation" and more than 4,000 families have no w.c.

At a time when we so often read about our affluent British society these facts come as a serious revelation to many people. We have grown so used to hearing about the Welfare State, so accustomed to seeing the bulldozers at work in our towns and cities that we have forgotten how much still remains to be done. One secondary schoolteacher wrote this about one of his pupils :

"George was an interesting boy. He was bronchitic, and had a fearful attendance record. Through contact with the welfare department I learned, quite by chance, that he had to sleep by the Ideal boiler in the kitchen/living room in a basement. There was one other room in the 'flat', and this, with a screen in it, served as bedroom for his two teenage sisters and his parents. When he used to fall asleep in the classroom, as he often did, I used to think of the previous evening, of the boy waiting for his parents to retire to their overcrowded room, so that he could himself get some rest—and I let him sleep."

Yet the effects of this chronically bad housing are not just physical. The cockroaches, the bed-bugs and the rats, the mouldering walls and the fungus are bad enough : but the overcrowding is, if anything, worse. It leads to tension and frustration, to shouting and screaming. Before long, it forces the younger children onto the streets and the older ones into delinquency. It leads to increasing strain and breakdown, and sometimes suicide, for the parents. It means infection and often serious illness. It makes homework impossible.

One teacher from North Kensington summed it all up like this :

"For ten years I have taught the adolescents of this twilight zone, and in that time I have witnessed a heart-breaking stream of lost opportunities, of lives ruined before they even started."

Both the main political parties, after studying this problem, stated that it would take at least ten years to cure homelessness and the worst of the overcrowding in Britain. Quite clearly many thousands of desperate families just could not wait that long. Some kind of first-aid operation was essential.

The National Campaign for the Homeless, better known by its short title, SHELTER, was set up to help meet this emergency. Rev. Bruce Kenrick, its chief instigator, already well known for his work in Notting Hill and for his book "Come Out the Wilderness" became Chairman of it. Christians from all walks of life and of every denomination came forward in support. Well known personalities in television, the musical world, the Church and politics agreed to act as sponsors. The British Churches Housing Trust, Christian Action, the Catholic Housing Aid Society and many other local housing associations started to work closely with it. Local SHELTER groups were formed in big cities and small villages and soon money was being raised in 36 counties of England, Scotland and Wales. Many helped by sponsoring young people in SHELTER walks, and agreeing to pay a fixed sum for each mile walked. And though the campaign was launched as recently as December, 1966, 750 people who had spent their Christmas in dank, crowded accommodation were re-housed by March 1967 with the money raised.

As soon as SHELTER receives gift money, it quickly distributes it to the various voluntary housing associations which are at work in our towns and cities. These housing associations are non-profit-making groups, and they can borrow large sums of money in addition to the gift money they get from SHELTER. All the money is used to buy houses (usually large ones) to repair and improve them if necessary, and then to let them at reasonable rents to needy families. The rents go to pay back the money which has been borrowed and since the housing associations are not out to make a profit, expenses are kept down.

This is the chief way in which SHELTER is working to clear the backlog of overcrowding and rebuilding in Britain today. By 1970 it hopes to be raising £1 million every year. Meantime the young, full-time team which carries out its day to day activities are thrusting ahead with publicity and propaganda designed to challenge their fellow men into support and action. As one leaflet puts it, "SHELTER starts where the gospel starts . . . with families in desperate need."

———— • ————

1. Why has it become necessary to mount a movement like SHEL-TER (National Campaign for the Homeless) in this country? Can the responsibility for homelessness be laid fairly at anyone's door? Discuss or debate these questions.
2. Write to the Social Responsibility Department of the British Council of Churches, 10 Eaton Gate, London, S.W.1 to find out what housing projects are being sponsored by religious bodies. If there is one in your area it may be possible to invite a representative to talk to your form about it.
3. SHELTER can use almost any offer of help. The full address is:
   SHELTER,
   National Campaign for the Homeless,
   86, The Strand,
   LONDON, W.C.2.
4. Find out all you can about any demolition or rebuilding schemes which have taken place in your nearest big town over the last ten years. Do you think any big mistakes have been made in the planning? If so, give reasons for your answer.

26   REFUGEES AND "BRACEROS"

At the beginning of 1966 the number of refugees in the world was estimated to be somewhere between six and ten million. Of that number approximately 867,000 were African, more than one and a quarter million were in Hong Kong, two million were in South-East Asia, two million in Southern Asia, several hundred thousand in Latin America and about 28,000 in Europe. This last small figure, as we have already mentioned in Chapter 20, is due largely to the success of World Refugee Year in 1959-60. Yet despite the relatively small numbers in Europe, refugees are still a world problem.

Every year the Refugee Service of the World Council of Churches resettles an average of about 12,000 refugees through its emigration programme. Some, however, are either too aged or too ill to start life again in a fresh country. For them, new accommodation is needed in the places where they now live. Every year the World Council accepts responsibility for some hundreds of these elderly or infirm refugees and places them in homes for the rest of their lives. For young refugees, who above all need the chance to learn a trade, training workshops have been equipped in several areas, including the Middle East and Hong Kong. Here they have learned the skills which later have made them acceptable immigrants in other countries.

Some people will point out straight away that the World Council's refugee work is only scratching the surface of a vast problem. Whilst this is in part true, the following four brief 'case histories' help to show what the Council's assistance means to those who actually receive it. Later on, in Chapter 32, we shall try to show how the World Council of Churches came to be formed. Suffice it to say here that it has a membership at the present time of some two hundred different Protestant denominations.

In 1966, the father of a Yugoslav refugee family living in Italy died. The mother was in poor health, but a grant from the World Council's Refugee Service enabled the daughter to pay to be trained as an interpreter. She qualified and so she was able to support her mother and the rest of her family. In Lebanon, a refugee was assisted in the purchase of an artificial limb so that he could go on earning his own living. In the Near East, one young man was in danger of going blind. A World Council grant enabled him not only to pay for an eye operation, which was successful, but also to take a period of vocational training afterwards. Lastly, a plumber who had been forced to flee from Europe was able, through help from the Refugee Service, to set up business in Chile.

These four examples help us to see the personal side of the World Council's work among refugees. Hundreds of similar cases could be cited.

106

Another important kind of work which the World Council of Churches undertakes is among migrant workers. Most people in Britain are familiar with one end of this problem because of the West Indian, Pakistani and Indian immigrants whomh we see in our big cities. In Britain today the number of immigrants is carefully controlled so that the situation should not be allowed to get out of hand. In three areas of the world, however, it has become a serious problem. Let us look at one of these three trouble spots.

In the last few years nearly 500,000 Bolivians have moved southwards to cross the border into Argentina. These Bolivian "braceros" (migrant workers) have flocked into the outskirts of Argentina's major cities. Nearly 200,000 of them spend a fifteen hour working day in temperatures ranging from 8 to 45 degrees centigrade. They quench their thirst with the waste water which runs through the ditches of the sugar plantations. Almost 100,000 of them lead a nomadic, wandering life from one harvest season to the next. Their children are born in the ploughed fields. Their dead are left by the side of the roads.

The Migration Department of the World Council of Churches has already begun to wrestle with this great problem. Early in 1966 it called all the Protestant Churches together to a consultation at Cochamba in Bolivia. The delegates decided immediately to alert every individual Church, and public opinion in general, about this question. A centre was set up on the Bolivia-Argentina border where the braceros could be informed and advised about their rights as Argentinian immigrants, and where they could obtain further information and, if necessary, emergency relief. Meanwhile, further action was carefully planned.

The Youth Department of the World Council has been anxious to help with the problems of these migrant workers as well as with those of the refugees. Each year it sponsors Youth Service Projects, and in 1966 there were 37 such projects supported by about 700 young people in 23 countries. These young men and women represented many different Christian denominations and the work they undertake is very varied. Sometimes it may mean working on a church or chapel building, or in the construction of a youth or community centre. Sometimes it means doing social work, sometimes helping to build houses.

One notable project was the long-term work camp in Korea which began in September 1965 and was wound up in June 1966. It attracted fifteen campers from ten countries representing five denominations. The first five months were spent in Taejon City, which has a population of 300,000. Terraces were dug in which crops could be planted and the students also helped the staff of an orphanage which cares for two hundred children. In December the campers moved on to the island of Koje (population 120,000) and laid the foundations for a centre which is to serve as a lecture hall for youth groups and young farmers in training. Here also they worked in a local orphanage and each camper "adopted" one of the children. They quickly became accepted as a part of the local community.

In some respects the work which the World Council of Churches does amongst refugees and migrant workers is disappointing. No sooner has the situation been eased in one trouble spot than tension and war in a new area cry out for help and emergency relief. It is work which goes on ceaselessly and without respite.

1. Does saying a prayer like "God bless refugees" make any difference? How can it help?

2. What ways can you suggest for ensuring that a greater share of our national wealth is devoted to work such as that among refugees?

3. Details of projects in hand to help refugees can be obtained from: The Division of Inter-Church Aid, Refugee, and World Service, World Council of Churches, Geneva.
   Study one of these projects in detail, and try to persuade your friends to do the same with other projects. Then compare notes.

27   THE POPULATION EXPLOSION

Way back in 1798 a young clergyman, T. R. Malthus, wrote a famous essay entitled "The Principles of Population as it Affects the Future Improvement of Society". In the essay Malthus showed that population increases by geometrical progression (i.e. 2, 4, 8, 16, 32 and so on) whereas the supply of food only increases by arithmetical progression (i.e. 2, 4, 6, 8, 10 and so on). A day would therefore come, he said, when the number of people waiting to be fed would far outstrip the amount of food available. That threat, which was forgotten for a hundred years or more because of the tremendous rise in food production in the nineteenth century, is now with us. It arises because of what has come to be called 'The Population Explosion'.

As this chapter is written, the population of the world is about 3,500 million people. Half of them were born *after* World War II. The increase since 1945 — nearly 1,700 millions — is roughly equal to what the population of the whole world was in the year 1900.

It took nearly the whole of human history (more than a million years) to produce the first thousand million (1,000,000,000) human beings, which was the total world population in the year 1830. To produce the next thousand million took only 100 years, until 1930. The third thousand million was born within the next thirty years up to 1960. From summer 1965 to summer 1966 there was a world population increase of 65 millions — or 180,000 people every day.

The main reason why the world's population is "exploding" at this rate is not that more children are being born, but that more are living to be adults instead of dying in infancy, as so many millions used to do. Years ago, almost everywhere in the world, one infant in every two died at birth. Today, in the Western countries, infant mortality is down to about twenty in every thousand, and even in the under-developed nations it is usually no higher than about 80 per thousand. Research into illness and disease has also cut down drastically the numbers of children who die in childhood. In other words, man has learnt how to prevent children dying, but he has not yet learnt how to control birth.

Of the world's 3,500 million people, about 1,500 million live in the under-developed countries. United Nations figures show that the population of these poorer countries has been increasing recently rather more than twice as fast as the population of Western Europe. In 1962, the average income per head of people living in these developing nations was less than £1 per week, whilst some of them (the 470 millions in India for instance) had an average income of less than 10/- per week. By contrast, the 340 million people in Western Europe had an average yearly income of £350 each, and the 205 millions in North America nearly three times that amount.

Some United Nations officials believe that it is possible to solve the basic problems of starvation, poverty and severe hardship in a comparatively short time. Even if this is achieved, however, many years of hard work will have to be put in before more than a handful of the under-developed nations can stand on their own feet.

Earlier in this book we saw in our study of the Masai Scheme and later of Oxfam that help is being given to the poorer countries in several different ways. Not only is food and money going to them, but also they are being helped to understand modern farming methods and simple agricultural science. We have also examined some of the ways in which the World Council of Churches is helping world poverty through its Refugee Department. Another way of helping to ease some of the world's problems must now be discussed — and that is to limit the increase of population by methods of birth control.

The most rapid population increases are taking place today in Asia, and especially in China and in India. In these primitive societies children are looked upon as a form of cheap labour and as a protection against poverty in old age. Fertility and the production of a large family are regarded as one of the greatest blessings of life. Again, many countries regard an increasing population as an insurance against war and as giving prestige value to the nation concerned. Further, the teachings of many of the world's religions are against any form of birth control, simply because it prevents life. The Hindu, for example, prizes life so highly that he resists attempts to destroy the animals which are ruining his crops and causing his family to go hungry. The reverence in India for the cow, which is considered to be a sacred animal, stands in the way of producing better cattle and more milk.

Among the Christians of the world there is a division of opinion on birth control. Up to now, the official teaching of the Roman Catholic Church has been that artificial methods of controlling birth are wrong, and against the law of God. Protestants, on the other hand, generally take a different view. Few of them oppose birth control, and many feel strongly that the Church should make it more widely known, especially to those who live in the under-developed countries. A new discovery such as the birth control pill, when it can be produced cheaply, should make it possible to limit the increase in population quite dramatically. For example, the birth control programme being introduced into Pakistan is expected to reduce the increase in that country's population over the next twenty years by no less than ninety million people!

There are good reasons, therefore, why missionaries in many

parts of the world are informing men and women about birth control. They do it because they know that unwanted children, especially when their parents are desperately poor, have little chance of finding any happiness in life. They believe that bringing into the world a smaller family, whose parents are able to feed and care for it properly, is nearer to Christ's teaching about 'loving one's neighbour' than having as many children as possible, regardless of the circumstances.

————————

1. Do you agree with the missionary who said that in a hungry world Christians have no right to have more than three children?
2. It has been said that one harvest which has not yet been fully reaped is the harvest of the sea. Find out all you can about 'farming' the oceans, as well as about other ways in which more food might be produced.
3. What is the United Nations Organisation at present doing under the following headings:
   (a) Food and agriculture (b) World Health?
   Suggest ways in which you believe more might be done.

28 THE CARE OF THE ELDERLY

Every day in Britain, 1,000 people reach retirement. Yet at the traditional retiring ages (60 for women and 65 for men), people are not nowadays regarded as old. Often they will continue to work part-time or perhaps take up some form of voluntary work, or find an interesting hobby or a new skill. Given reasonable health, retirement offers many attractive possibilities. As someone has said "It is no longer regarded as the beginning of the end, but as the end of the beginning of life."

Due largely to the fact that people live longer these days, the number of old people in Britain is increasing fairly rapidly. Today, one out of every nine people in this country is over 65 — in all, about 6½ million men and women. Of this number, about 300,000 live in institutions. By 1979 the total number of elderly persons in Great Britain is likely to be about 9,500,000, or 18.2 per cent of the population.

Accommodation is going to be a big problem for these growing numbers of old people. It has been estimated that 75,000 new dwellings will be required for Britain's pensioners every year for the next twenty years! Whereas many old people today are unable to continue living in their own homes unless they have special assistance, a "purpose built" flat or bungalow can often help them to remain independent for several years longer. Many local churches are now acquiring property for old people along these lines.

The needs of the elderly, however, can often be met in much smaller ways. Routine tasks which a younger person can do in a few minutes may take an old person several hours to complete. Young people, like the Community Service Volunteers, are helping with jobs like shopping, window-cleaning, gardening, filling in forms, changing library books and home decoration.

The longer they live, of course, the greater the needs of elderly people are likely to be. Friends and relatives of a similar age are often dead : there may be no younger relations, and if there are

they may live a great distance away. So it is that very often lone-liness becomes a real problem. About one and a half million, mainly elderly women, live alone (twice as many as 30 years ago) and about 675,000 old people are housebound.

Many elderly people who have nobody but themselves to look after find it too much of an effort to go shopping and then cook properly balanced meals for themselves. Some of them, 'making do' for months or even years with cheap tinned food or with a diet made up mainly of bread and potatoes, suffer from acute anaemia and sometimes even from malnutrition. Yet there may be a friend or a neighbour coming into the house every day. For many years now, the Meals on Wheels Scheme has provided a hot midday meal at least twice a week for thousands of old people. The meals are usually cooked at a centre and are then delivered in heated con-

114

tainers either by van or private car. Usually consisting of meat, two vegetables and a sweet, they are subsidised by local authorities and the old people pay on average about 1s. 6d. each for them. Over nine million of these meals are being delivered each year to the elderly in more than 1,800 areas, and new centres are continually being opened.

The Meals on Wheels Scheme is one of the biggest jobs being undertaken by the Women's Royal Voluntary Service today. These ladies, the "Women in Green" have been part of Britain's national life since 1938. Some of the tasks which they were doing before the war have now been taken over by the government, but there is still a vast amount of urgent social work to be done. Whilst the Meals on Wheels Scheme is intended mainly for elderly people who are housebound, W.R.V.S. encourages those who are able to get about to go to one of its luncheon clubs. The old people themselves often help in serving the meals and in washing up afterwards and they much enjoy their lunchtime outings.

W.R.V.S. runs many other clubs for elderly people also. It has opened nearly a hundred "All Day" clubs. Here, members pay a weekly subscription of 3d. or 6d. and they can then use the clubs to read, chat, play games, work at various handicrafts or just sit in a warm, pleasant room. Often facilities for saving are provided and money can be put aside for day outings, Christmas shopping, and so on.

In addition to these All Day Clubs, W.R.V.S. runs twenty-three residential clubs for old people. Should nursing care be needed, there are two nursing homes as well. W.R.V.S. has sponsored over 2,000 of the well known Darby and Joan clubs, which provide a bright spot for many thousands of old people on one afternoon each week.

The Spare a Mile Scheme (usually known as SAM) is one which any motorist with a car can join. W.R.V.S. puts willing drivers in touch with old folk who may not have been out for years, and who would like to visit a friend in hospital, or perhaps to go to church or for a run in the country. The motorists decide what mileage they are prepared to give each month and their names and addresses are then put on a list at the local W.R.V.S. Centre.

Though its work is by no means confined to care of the elderly,

W.R.V.S. works in a variety of other ways to help old people. For example, it pioneered the Home Help Service, now taken over by the local authorities. Under this scheme, domestic help is made available for an hour or more each week to needy cases. Often the service is provided at reduced rates, and sometimes it is given free. W.R.V.S. provides escorts for frail elderly persons when they have to visit hospital. In certain cases it arranges for regular visitation of the housebound. In these and a multitude of other ways it seeks to serve those no longer young.

Each year the growing numbers of Britain's old people provide new problems. Each year W.R.V.S. contributes help and human kindness for their solution.

1. 'Grow old along with me!
   The best is yet to be,
   The last of life, for which the first was made;
   Our times are in His hand
   Who saith, 'A whole I planned,
   Youth shows but half; trust God; see all nor be afraid!'
   (Robert Browning)
   Discuss the poem. How does Christian faith help us to believe that the first two lines of it are true, (i) for this life, (ii) for what lies beyond it?

2. *Opportunity for Service* (price 6d. post free) lists over one hundred ways in which young people in the 15-20 age-group may undertake community service. It is obtainable from:
   King George's Jubilee Trust,
   166 Piccadilly,
   LONDON, W.1.

3. Could God's plan for the life of a man or woman ever include senility?

116

29   SOMETHING FOR NOTHING

Gambling is growing in Britain today. It has become an important feature of our national life, and all the signs are that it will go on increasing in volume in the years to come. Whether we are happy with this state of affairs or not, we must examine the facts about gambling and then decide personally what our attitude to it is going to be.

It is difficult to get exact figures for the total amount of money spent on gambling, but Table 1 gives some indication of the extent of its growth in Britain recently.

Table 1

GAMBLING TURNOVER (To the nearest £5 million)	1960	1961	1962	1963	1964	1965
Horseracing*	385	440	540	560	600	610
Greyhound Racing	125	125	115	110	110	125
Football Pools	110	100	85	70	85	100
Fixed Odds Football Betting	45	50	60	65	45	15
Bingo in Commercial Clubs		25	30	35	35	35
Premium Bonds (Interest Lottery)	10	15	15	20	20	20
Other Forms (Fun-Fairs, etc.)	5	5	10	10	10	10
TOTAL	680	760	855	870	905	915

* The turnover may be considerably in excess of this figure

Table 2

BRITAIN'S NATIONAL CONSUMER EXPENDITURE (£ millions)	1964	1965
Food	5,557	5,765
Housing	2,106	2,447
Clothing and Footwear	1,919	2,034
Tobacco	1,344	1,429
Alcoholic Drink	1,316	1,417
Cars, Motor-cycles, Radio and Electrical Goods	1,278	1,323
Fuel and Light	978	1,090
Furniture and Floor Coverings	486	510
Other Goods and Services	6,054	6,638
TOTAL	21,038	22,653

We can see how it compares with other national expenditure by looking at Table 2. Thus, for example, by comparing the two Tables we notice that in 1965 total Gambling Turnover in Britain was almost half of the amount spent on clothing and footwear that year. Table 1 shows that since 1960 some forms of gambling have actually decreased, whilst one in particular has grown greatly.

What exactly do we mean by gambling ? In this country today it means betting, gaming and lotteries. In betting, those who are taking part lay a wager, or bet, on what the result of a game or an event will be. Thus you can bet with a friend or bet with a book-maker on all kinds of sporting and other events. Gaming, on the other hand, is the playing of a game of chance (or of chance and

118

skill combined), for stakes. Roulette is a game of chance, whereas bridge is a game of chance and skill combined. Lotteries depend on the drawing of tickets or "lots". The tickets are usually sold at a uniform price and the prizes derive from the stakes. The winning tickets are selected by chance — perhaps by drawing from a hat, perhaps from a machine. A raffle and a sweepstake are both examples of a lottery.

Sometimes it seems difficult to decide what is a gamble and what is not. How, then, can we define a gamble? The best definition we have contains five distinct features, and it is this: "Gambling is (1) a redistribution of wealth, (2) on the basis of an artificially created risk, (3) involving gain, without service rendered, for one party, (4) at the loss of another party, (5) on an appeal to chance." All five of these features must be present together before we have a true gamble — and the definition draws a clear line in such a way that all gambles, and only gambles, fall on one side of it.

Why do people gamble? Most people, if they were asked that question would probably use the title of this chapter and reply "To get something for nothing". Certainly for many gamblers the hope of winning money is the principal motive. But there are also many gamblers for whom the "thrill" of the gamble is more important than the thought of actually winning money. For these men and women it is the excitement which is the attraction.

We should not make the mistake of thinking that gamblers in this second category are all people whose lives are dull and dreary or whose homes are unhappy. Many of the most regular gamblers in this group are men with happy homes, satisfying jobs and very often a good income as well.

Sometimes a regular, habitual gambler becomes a compulsive one. Usually compulsive gamblers are from the second ("thrill and excitement") group. Only rarely are they women. Very little is known as yet about the reasons why this happens. What is clear is that a compulsive gambler is a sick man, and that he retreats into a dream world of his own. He now becomes firmly convinced that he can justify himself and beat all the odds which are ranged against him. Soon his compulsion begins to affect every part of his life. He loses his friends. His home life is affected. He begs, borrows and ultimately even steals so as to find money with which to gamble.

Eventually the time comes when there is nobody left from whom he can borrow. His debts are vast. He has lost his home and his family. He may then attempt suicide.

Gamblers Anonymous (or G.A.), was founded in 1964 to help compulsive gamblers back to recovery. The organisation began in America and it is based on the methods and principles of Alcoholics Anonymous. Meetings are held every week and the members are invited to talk about their own experiences. Sometimes a psychiatrist is there to offer help and advice. But the greatest help usually comes from listening to the various members of the group itself. Sometimes they talk about the new life they have made since they gave gambling up, sometimes about their gambling days. And as each one tells his story, the others in the group hear a tale very similar indeed to their own.

For many compulsive gamblers Gamblers Anonymous, with its various branches in London and the provinces, provides the gateway to a new way of living. It is a non-sectarian organisation, and is not committed to any particular religious beliefs, but the recovery programme is based upon acceptance of certain spiritual values. For example, most members of G.A. believe in the existence of what the groups call a 'Power' greater than themselves.

It has been said that apart from Gamblers Anonymous there is, for the compulsive gambler, only the gutter, the river, or prison. Unfortunately, it cannot be claimed that Gamblers Anonymous succeeds in every 'case'. The failure rate is high, and quite often men lapse back into gambling habits. Sometimes they come back again to Gamblers Anonymous : often they do not. In order to help, a parallel organisation for the families of sufferers, called Gam-Anon, has been set up.

Undoubtedly the phenomenal rise in gambling since 1960 is due in some measure to the Betting and Gaming Act passed in that year. The Act provided for licensed betting offices, and for the legalisation of gaming, subject to three clear regulations. Unfortunately it has led to more widespread gambling than was intended. The thousands of bingo and gaming clubs which have sprung up since 1960 are due to faulty wording in the Act. Many other ways round the legislation have also been discovered.

The Churches Council on Gambling has been studying the

problems that gambling creates for many years. It is concerned not so much to condemn gambling, as to try to discover the reasons why people want to gamble. The figures which it compiles are used by both the government and the Press. From time to time it carries out research with Universities into the causes and effects of gambling, and publishes the results. But above all it is concerned to alleviate the misery and hardship which come to families when one, or even both parents, gamble compulsively.

1. "If people intend to do good with their money it does not matter how they come by it." Debate this statement.
2. Is there a difference between an adventure and a gamble? Is Christianity either? Write down your views on this question.
3. Useful addresses:
   The Churches Council on Gambling, and Gamblers Anonymous, although separate organisations, are both housed at:
   19 Abbey House,
   Victoria Street,
   LONDON, S.W.1.
4. Does a lottery, sponsored by a government, make gambling *more* moral?

30   CRIMES OF VIOLENCE
AND YOUNG OFFENDERS

Crime is rising in Britain today, and the increase seems to be most marked in the under-21 age-group. An upward trend has been noticed for some years now and all the signs are that it will continue in the immediate future. But the problem is not confined to Britain alone. In nearly every country which has had marked improvement in its material prosperity, there seems to have been a substantial increase in crime, and especially in juvenile cases.

No one really knows just how much crime there is. The Criminal Statistics for England and Wales which are issued each year give details of the crimes known to the police, but they take no account of undiscovered offences. Table One and Table Two below have been taken from these statistics and they show us that in 1966 there were 1,199,859 indictable offences known to the police, whereas in 1960 there were 743,713 and in 1950 only 461,435.

Table 1

Year	INDICTABLE OFFENCES KNOWN TO THE POLICE			
	Breaking and Entering	Sexual Offences	Violence against the Person	TOTAL
1950	92,839	13,185	6,249	461,435
1955	74,907	17,078	7,884	438,085
1960	151,378	19,937	15,759	743,713
1966	275,969	21,308	26,716	1,199,859

NOTE: The total number of indictable offences topped the million mark for the first time in 1964. (1,067,963 offences)

Table 2

Ages	BREAKDOWN BY AGE OF MALES FOUND GUILTY OF INDICTABLE OFFENCES				
	1950	1964	1965	1966	% Variation 1966 over 1965
under 14	24,521	22,786	22,376	21,648	minus 3·3
14—17	14,624	32,796	32,818	32,948	plus 0·4
17—21	10,940	35,750	40,486	45,243	plus 11·7
21—30	21,855	42,737	47,099	52,938	plus 12·4
30 plus	29,008	42,406	44,645	48,681	plus 9·0
TOTAL	100,948	176,475	187,424	201,458	plus 7·5

"Indictable" offences mean those which may be tried by a jury — usually the more serious crimes. Violence against the person (which includes murder, manslaughter and wounding), breaking and entering, sexual offences and most forms of larceny (the legal term for stealing) are all examples of indictable offences.

"Non-indictable" offences (sometimes called "petty offences") include most of the less serious offences such as breaches of traffic and parking regulations, and these are usually tried before the local magistrates. (It is worth noting that of the people in Britain found guilty of all offences in 1966, 65 per cent had broken one or other of the traffic laws!)

123

It is the enormous increase in recent years in the number of indictable offences which is especially causing concern in Britain today. Crimes of violence against the person, for example, were more than four times as great in 1966 as they were in 1950. Breaking and entering has increased nearly threefold in the same period, from 92,839 cases in 1950 to 275,969 in 1966. Sexual offences in 1966 were one and a half times greater than they were in 1950 — and so we might go on, listing other categories of serious crime.

In 1966, 232,854 men and women were convicted and found guilty of indictable offences. Of that number only 31,396 were females. The vast majority, 201,458, were males — and if we break that figure down we find that less than one quarter of them were over 30. Roughly a quarter were between 21 and 30, nearly a quarter were between 17 and 21 and over a quarter (54,596) under 17. Of those 54,596 boys, 32,948 were between 14 and 17 and 21,648 under 14.

What makes a young person turn to crime ? What kind of boys and girls are today's young offenders, and from what kind of homes do they usually come ? A wide range of people tries to answer these questions and they quote their own pet theories to account for the increasing rate of crimes. But the straight answer is this : at the moment no one knows much about why young people (or, for that matter, older ones) commit crime, or why some criminals later decide to go straight. One thing is absolutely clear : there is no single cause which is mainly responsible for the increase.

Investigators are fairly sure about some of the probable causes. The low rate of detection and conviction, for instance (with only 40 per cent of those 1,199,859 indictable offences cleared up in 1966) makes some people much more willing to "have a go". Increased national affluence leads to more opportunities to commit crime. Other probable causes include the influence of broken homes, the increase in the amount of 'violence' shown on television and in the cinema, and the fact that many magistrates seem reluctant to make full use of existing penalties when dealing with young as well as older offenders.

In Britain today a boy may be given a conditional discharge by the Court after his first offence. Alternatively, he may be put on probation or sent to a Detention Centre. If he is between 15 and 21 he may be sent for Borstal training. If he is over 17 he may be fined or sent to prison. And whether he is imprisoned or not, a whole range of people and organisations, of whom the Probation Officer is only one, will help him to go straight if he is prepared to work with them. But more and more the police, the prisoners' organisations, the churches and others are realising that "after-care", good though it may be, is only a second-best solution. The most important thing of all is to *prevent* crime.

A lot of thought has been given to crime prevention in the United States of America, where juvenile delinquency is even more serious than in this country. In New York since 1961 and now in several other big American cities, including Chicago, a courageous series of experiments is going on. These experiments are called Teen Challenge.

Late in 1960 David Wilkerson, a young country minister who had moved to New York from Pennsylvania, persuaded some of his friends to join him in buying what looked from the outside like a stately, red-brick Georgian house. It was in Clinton Avenue, Brooklyn, New York. But though the exterior looked like a mansion, the inside was a shambles. Piled high with old newspapers, broken bottles and other accumulated junk, the house had been unoccupied for two years. Most of the water pipes were fractured, the ceilings and walls needed re-plastering, doors had been ripped away from their hinges and the bannister rails lolled on their side. A work-party of teenagers cleared that great house room by room and floor by floor until every bit of rubbish and junk had been finally tipped out. Then painters and plumbers, electricians and joiners moved in, and by late spring 1961 the Teen Challenge Centre was in full swing.

In addition to David Wilkerson and his family twenty young men and women live in the Centre. They are volunteers, and they have come to Brooklyn to learn how to talk to the teenage gangs of Harlem and the Bronx, and of Brooklyn itself. They spend each morning in study and in prayer — and the study includes not only a knowledge of the Bible but also of the symptoms of drug addiction and alcoholism. Then after lunch, the street day begins. These twenty young people go out in twos and threes, walking over prescribed routes and keeping an eye open for signs of trouble.

Sometimes they visit jails and hospitals, schools and courts. But especially they make it their business to talk to members of the New York gangs, particularly the fighting gangs like the Suicides and the Cobras. Some of the boys and girls they meet who are on drugs are so ill that they are brought to live in the Centre until they are well again. But many can be helped on the spot, and one of the most impressive results of the work of Teen Challenge in New York has been that over these last years several hundreds of youngsters have left their gangs and have been helped back to a normal way of living.

Some of those hundreds have become professing Christians, and are now leading useful and profitable lives. A few have themselves joined in the work of Teen Challenge and have gone out to the streets, often in peril of their lives. Meanwhile, David Wilkerson and his friends, backed now by some of the most influential business men in the United States, are watching the work of Teen Challenge grow day by day, as new chapters are written in the changed lives of teenagers all over New York.

————◆————

1. What do you think are the reasons why juvenile crime is increasing? What can be done to combat this increase?
2. Read carefully the story of how Jesus cleared the Temple Court. Do you think this is an example of 'violence'?
3. You can read the full story of Teen Challenge in *The Cross and the Switchblade* by David Wilkerson (Spire Books).
4. Is the use of physical force ever justifiable? If so, under what circumstances? If not, say why.

31   COLOUR IN BRITAIN

There have always been some coloured people living in Britain. In the 1920's and the 1930's, however, their numbers increased quite appreciably and they began to settle down together in big cities such as London, Manchester and Birmingham. After the Second World War increasing numbers of them — mainly West Indians, Indians and Pakistanis came to this country. When they arrived, most of them went to live near their fellow-countrymen in places like Moss Side, Manchester and Hyde Park, Leeds. It seemed likely that if their numbers went on growing unchecked there might be serious racial trouble and so the government eventually began to control immigration. Today there are about a million coloured people in Britain. Our total population is about fifty-five millions.

The relationship between different races is a problem in many countries of the world today. In the United States, for instance, where Africans were originally brought in to work as slaves on the cotton plantations, there is bitterness and hatred between black and white. Yet there is also serious trouble where no black or white faces are involved. Racial conflict exists in South East Asia and in India, where Chinese, Polynesians and Indians often live and work side by side. In Ceylon there is frequently racial tension between the Sinhalese and the Tamils. By contrast, in Brazil, several different races have settled down together happily, and they are an example to the rest of the world.

At one time the different races of the world were more or less separated from each other — sometimes by a range of mountains, sometimes by the sea. Today, communication between one part of the world and another is much swifter. Not only the airways of the world, but also radio and television, have made the earth seem much smaller. And as this process goes on, multi-racial nations, containing many different colours and many different creeds, are appearing. Britain, at one time practically cut off from the rest of the world by water, is one of them.

Coloured people already play an important part in the day-to-day life of our nation. We have become used to seeing West Indians and Pakistanis working on our buses and trains. If you are rushed off to hospital in the middle of the night for an emergency operation, the chances are that it will be performed by an Indian or Pakistani doctor and that you will be looked after by a West Indian Nurse. If a blood transfusion is needed, it is quite possible that the blood of a coloured donor will be used in an attempt to save your life. And it is experiences like this which make us realise, as scientists have so often told us, that it is only the colour of our skin which varies : underneath we are all exactly the same. No one race or colour is inferior in either physical, mental or spiritual powers to any other.

Now Christians agree with all this, but not just because science says so. They believe that all men are equal simply because, being children of God, they are all members of his family. If the human race is to survive in this nuclear age, the members of that family must learn to live and work side by side with each other.

Why, and how, does racial discrimination begin ? As long as there were only a few thousand coloured immigrants in Britain spread thinly, as a rule, throughout the slums of our big cities, nobody much seemed to mind them being there at all. But when in the 1950's much larger numbers arrived, trouble started. For some of these immigrants were ambitious. They wanted to succeed in their work, and so they started to apply for better jobs. They wanted to acquire better houses, so some of them began to move out from the slums into the suburbs. And soon, often because of clever propaganda, white people began to fear not only for the value of their property, but also for their jobs. Despite this, cases of colour discrimination seem to have been very uncommon until about 1958. But in that year and the years following, there was a series of racial disturbances, mainly in London but also in provincial cities such as Nottingham. It was obvious that a barrier had grown up in Britain between white and coloured people.

The National Committee for Commonwealth Immigrants, set up by the Prime Minister in September 1965, exists to help destroy that barrier. Its membership includes people from all parts of Britain and the Commonwealth. Its Chairman is the Archbishop of Canterbury, though it is not connected with any specific religious body.

In working in every possible way "for the elimination of race prejudice in the United Kingdom", N.C.C.I. has a wide influence. For example, it advises the government on all questions relating to immigration — and it told the Prime Minister in 1965 that government immigration policies had done considerable harm to the cause of integration. It also brings together employers, trade unionists and others to discuss fair employment practices. It publishes reports and pamphlets on problems like integration and community relations, and it trains social workers, teachers and others to deal with them. The nine panels of specialists who advise the Council cover, amongst others, the fields of housing, education, health and welfare, and legal affairs.

Much of the practical work, however, which is done in local communities cannot be tackled by a national committee. Voluntary liaison committees have therefore been set up in many areas throughout Britain to deal with local problems which affect everyone. The N.C.C.I. advises and assists these local liaison committees as their work develops, and often provides a grant towards the salary of a full-time secretary.

The Manchester liaison committee, which is known as the Manchester Council for Community Relations, appointed its first Community Liaison Officer in January, 1967. An Indian, he obtained two degrees at the University of Patna as well as a postgraduate Diploma of an English University. Prior to taking up work with the Council he had been employed as a personnel officer in industry.

The Council has formed various committees which meet at regular intervals, and some of their early discussions centred round slum clearance, rehousing and the possibility of setting up a Housing Association; the health problems of immigrants; the employment of Sikhs on buses; the problems of school leavers and special educational courses for immigrants.

At the social level, the Council has held dances and socials and now provides speakers on a fairly wide variety of topics to organisations in both the immigrant and host communities. Meantime, the University of Manchester has set up a Language Bank of people who can speak foreign languages and English fluently, in order to provide interpreting services whenever and wherever needed.

The N.C.C.I. cannot end all racial prejudice and discrimination in Britain today, simply because it does not claim to be able to change men's hearts. But where violence or injustice occur because of the colour of a man's skin, it is pledged to take action.

1.   Another organisation which has been working along similar lines is CARD (Campaign Against Racial Discrimination). Its National Headquarters is housed at 23 St. George's House, Toynbee Hall, Commercial Street, London, E.1., though, as with N.C.C.I. there is a strong regional organisation.

2.   "I'd accept a coloured man as my brother, but not as my brother-in-law . . . ."
     "God is black, a beautiful shining black. It is a wicked white man's lie to say he is white. The Devil is white." (A Nigerian student in London quoted in the *Geographical Magazine*, Jan. 1959).
     "You can play some sort of a tune on the white notes alone, and you can play some sort of a tune on the black notes alone: but to get harmony you must play black and white together." (Kwegyir Aggrey).   Consider the implications of these three statements.

3.   Collect as many examples as you can of prejudice shown between white and coloured people. From what basic causes do you think this prejudice springs?

4.   "Patterns of worship, church organisation and Christian education may need increasingly to be rethought and modified in the face of advancing racial inter-relationships." Discuss what practical steps your local church could take in this direction.

32   GETTING TOGETHER

It is nearly two thousand years now since the first followers of Jesus last listened to him speaking and preaching by Lake Galilee. Suddenly they realised that they must carry on without being able to ask his advice or guidance on their problems. Sad though they were about that, however, they were men and women of the future and not of the past. Jesus had told them: "Go into all the world and preach the gospel." They could do no less.

What were those early Christians like, and what form did their first "services" take? We know that most of them were ordinary people like ourselves. We know too that because their religion was so much hated by the authorities they often had to meet in secret and in fear of their lives. Whenever possible they held their meetings in one another's homes. Those early churches were "house" churches — and the worship was plain and simple. This was before anyone had considered it necessary to put up a special building and call it a "church" or "chapel", and even before the practice of singing hymns at services was introduced. The term "church" originally meant the group of Christians living and worshipping in a particular district.

Bit by bit, however, this simple way of worshipping altered. To begin with, the services took on a more fixed pattern. Certain words and sayings, for instance, began to be repeated at every service. Also, it became common to have a special room or building set apart for worship. And as the years passed, things became even more complicated.

As the Christian Church grew and spread, it split. The bishop of Rome (called Pope, or "father" by his people) claimed to speak for the Churches of Asia Minor and Greece ; however, the leader there, who was known as the Patriarch and lived in Constantinople, challenged the Pope's claim. In 1054 the quarrels came to a head and the Eastern (or Orthodox) and Roman (or Western) halves of the Church separated.

Nearly five hundred years later, on November 1st, 1517, Martin Luther, a dissatisfied Roman Catholic priest, nailed a list of 95 theses (or complaints) to the door of the Church in Wittenberg, Germany. By so doing Luther fired a spark which led to what is now called the Reformation. Because of it, many Christians broke away from the Roman Church and began to worship together in different, often more simple ways. The Church of England dates from this time, but other denominations like Lutherans, Congregationalists and Baptists were also established during this period. Often there was great bitterness and bloodshed between these new "Protestants", as they later became known, and Roman Catholics. The split of 1054 and the later splits of the Reformation and afterwards divided the Church very seriously. Today, many of those divisions still remain. The world's 940 million Christians are still divided up into 572 million Roman Catholics, 142 million Orthodox Christians, and 226 million Protestants.

In a world as troubled and confused as ours is, these divisions among Christian people are a scandal. Even more serious, as missionaries have gone out to China, India, Africa and other mission fields they have felt that they must bring converts into their own denomination, and so the divisions have been "exported". At times there has been overlapping in missionary work between Protestants and Catholics, and so the developing nations have heard different versions of the gospel.

Fortunately, there have always been some Christians working to draw the various Churches closer together but it was not until 1910 that a real step forward was made. In that year a missionary conference was held in Edinburgh, and it is from that date that the movement for closer fellowship between the Churches (or the ecumenical movement) dates. Most of the delegates at Edinburgh were from churches in Europe and America, but when similar conferences were held later abroad, a majority of the members came from the newer churches of India, Japan, China and Africa.

Following one of these conferences in 1937 the World Council of Churches was planned. After the war, in 1948, the Council was finally constituted at Amsterdam. Today, the World Council of Churches links together more than two hundred different sects, Anglican and Protestant.

Valuable though the work of the World Council is among Protestants of different denominations, there was until recently very little exchange between the three main divisions in the Christian Church. Then in 1960 Dr. Geoffrey Fisher, at that time Archbishop of Canterbury, paid a friendly visit to the Pope in Rome. Other Christians, Orthodox as well as Protestant, followed Dr. Fisher's example in the years which followed. Gradually it became clear that a thaw was taking place in the relations between the three main groupings of Christians.

When Pope John XXIII, whom Dr. Fisher visited, became Pope in 1958, he was already a very old man. It was said that many of the cardinals had voted for him simply because they thought he would be a good "caretaker". Yet they were in for a surprise, for Pope John's effect on the Roman Catholic Church was immediate, and it was electric! He spoke about wanting to open the windows of the Church so that fresh air and ideas could come in. In January 1959 he mentioned that he was going to call together in Rome a great Vatican Council to which representatives would come from almost every corner of the world. By the time that Council was finally sent home in December 1965 Pope John was dead, but the effects of "Vatican II" will be felt for years to come. Already, as a result of it. Roman Catholics in many countries are hearing parts of the Communion Service (or Mass) in their native language for the first time, instead of in Latin. Already the bishops are sharing more fully in Church affairs than before. And perhaps most important of all, a new enthusiasm for unity amongst all Christians is spreading throughout the Roman Catholic Church.

Meanwhile the Protestant Churches have also been drawing closer together. The Church of South India was brought into being by the union of Anglicans, Presbyterians, Congregationalists and Methodists. In Ceylon and in North India similar schemes for unity are well advanced. At home here in Britain several exciting developments are taking place. The Congregational Church in England and Wales and the Presbyterian Church of England hope to unite by 1970. The Church of England and the Methodist Church are also planning for unity with one another and are studying draft schemes. And lastly, at a gathering in 1964 of various denominations, great enthusiasm was expressed for unity and the conference called upon the Churches to try, if possible, to achieve it by 1980.

Nobody can tell at the moment how long it will be before the unity of all Christians is achieved. Certain it is that until it has come about the world will continue to be puzzled by the divisions amongst the Churches. Without unity, the title of this book can make only partial sense.

1. Is it absurd to set a target date such as 1980 for the achievement of unity of the Churches in Britain?
2. The British Council of Churches, 10 Eaton Gate, London, S.W.1 has Departments dealing with Social Responsibility, Youth, Christian Aid, Education and International Affairs. Choose the Department which interests you most and then write for full details about the scope of its work.
3. If Jesus came back on earth as a man, would he find he could use the Churches—or pass them by?
4. Make a list of the various Churches in your area, and find out in what ways, if any, they co-operate with one another. If they form a local Council of Churches, it may be possible to invite the Secretary of the Council to talk about its work.

33 IONA—THE CHURCH AND INDUSTRY

Iona is an island. It lies off the west coast of Scotland, separated from the Isle of Mull by a stretch of water about a mile broad. It is about three miles long from north to south and measures about a mile and a half at its widest point. Indescribably beautiful, it attracts tourist steamers in the calm days of summer, but it knows also days of storm and raging seas. Throughout the seasons and the centuries Iona has remained unchanged.

For as long as men can remember Iona has been a holy place. Saint Columba came to Iona from Ireland in 563 A.D. and in the years following his arrival men went out as missionaries to the islands nearby and later to the North of England. In this Celtic period kings came to worship on Iona, and some still lie buried there.

During the Middle Ages the Roman Church took over Iona, and it was during this time that the buildings now to be seen on the island were built. There were Benedictine monks in the Abbey then and there was also a Nunnery. But at the time of the Reformation the monasteries were suppressed. The last monks went away, and though there was no vandalism, the buildings gradually fell into decay.

In the 19th century Iona was owned by the Dukes of Argyll, but when the 8th Duke died in 1899 he bequeathed the island and its ruined buildings to the Church of Scotland. He expressed the wish that they might be restored, and also the hope that other Christian denominations might be allowed to hold services in them.

The next part of our story takes place in the 1930's, for during those difficult years Scotland, like England, was experiencing widespread unemployment. Govan, near Glasgow, was one of the worst hit areas. George MacLeod had come to be minister in Govan in 1930. During his eight years there he had seen the Church grow. It was well attended and active. It had opened clubs for the unemployed people of Govan. A youth hostel had been started. Many poor families had been given practical help. Yet George MacLeod was not satisfied. For all its apparent success, he believed his church was failing in its task. Those who attended the services on Sundays were not the men and women who worked in the factories and mills of industrial Govan. Despite all the social work the church was doing in the district, the bulk of the people in the parish were not being attracted into it. And what was true for his church was true also for the other churches which he knew. Something had gone seriously wrong.

In 1938 MacLeod gave up his post as minister of the church at Govan. He and his friends had planned very carefully what they wanted to do. They knew that for many people "Church" and "Christianity" meant something which happens on a Sunday and can then be conveniently forgotten for the rest of the week. They knew that ordinary men and women often feel embarrassed in the

George MacLeod on Iona.

company of a priest or minister. They knew, too, that many ministers find it difficult to talk to factory or mill workers, simply because they have never earned their living by working with their hands. In short, they realised only too well that the Church and the community outside had become separated. There was "the sacred" and "the secular" — and a barrier a mile high between them. Yet Jesus had known no such division. The things he had taught had to do with the *whole* of life — not just with Sunday morning and evening.

That is why a little group set sail for Iona in 1938, and how the Iona Community came to be formed. If only ministers and manual workers could live, and work and worship together — they could perhaps show how the Church and the outside world might come to be part of one another again.

At the beginning the Community consisted of only eight men. Half were craftsmen. The other half were young ministers of the Church of Scotland who had just finished their training. But they were not to remain on the island for the rest of their lives. The Iona Community was not to be another monastery. For after spending the summer months on the island, the members were to split up and go back again to their jobs on the mainland. There, day by day, they would try to put into practice what they had learnt on Iona. That is what in fact happened — and that is the plan which is still followed today.

In 1938 there were many people who thought that the attempt of a handful of men to rebuild a ruined monastery was completely senseless. But the work was begun, despite many conflicting opinions and much opposition.

When war came in 1939 workers were soon scarce . . . and so was timber. Then, almost miraculously, it seemed, a ship bound from Canada for Liverpool ran into rough seas and abandoned her cargo of wood in order to reach safety. The timber was washed up on the rocks of the Ross of Mull and the Community was able to rescue it and was given permission to keep it. That wood proved to be sufficient to roof a section of the building which had just been rebuilt !

From those small beginnings in the war years, the work of rebuilding Iona has gone on steadily. All but one of the medieval Abbey buildings are now restored. And each year, the members of the Community have been joined by new recruits who have come to spend their months on Iona and then gone back to their normal occupations on the mainland.

Young people have not been forgotten. Each summer, some six hundred of them aged from seventeen to thirty, and mainly from industrial areas, come to Youth Camps on the island for study and recreation. Some have later become full members of the Iona Community. Many have subsequently become Associate Members or Friends of Iona.

As the Duke of Argyll had hoped, Christians of many denominations come to Iona today, and feel at home. Though the Abbey belongs to the Church of Scotland, any Christian denomination is free to conduct services there according to its own rites. The Community itself now numbers about one hundred and fifty full members, and is made up of men representing many different Churches. But perhaps the most exciting thing of all is that through what is happening on Iona the Church is never able to forget about industry — or industry about the Church. Jesus the Craftsman and Worker, who spent nearly twenty years at a carpenter's bench before ever he began to preach and teach — this is the Christ that Iona exists to remind Scotland and the world about.

———————◆———————

1. Do you agree that the Churches today have very little contact with working-class people? If so, what practical suggestions can you make for meeting the problem?
2. If there is an industrial chaplain in your area it may be possible to invite him to come and discuss his work with you.
3. The Iona Community, 214 Clyde Street, Glasgow, C.1., have several publications and pamphlets covering their work. Read as many as you can.

CHRISTIANITY
AND OTHER RELIGIONS

Our world today, with its rapid communications and transport, is a "shrinking" world. Through a news item on radio or T.V., we can be put into immediate touch with the problems facing a nation thousands of miles away. Visitors from the four corners of the earth step down every day at London airport — some for a short stay only, some to make their homes in Britain and to spend the rest of their lives here.

This increasing movement of people from one country to another means that contact between men and women of different faiths is much more frequent than it used to be. Whereas at one time most of the information about other religions was given by missionaries when they came home on leave, today, through immigration, we can find a Sikh temple or a Buddhist shrine in several English towns.

Another important factor for all religions, including Christianity, is the effect of education and the spread of science and technology. Much of the mystery about the natural world has been removed as man has come to learn more about it, and the hold of religion over the lives of millions of people has been weakened. Thunder, lightning, storm and flood are no longer inexplicable mysteries, and medicine can now provide a cure where previously a magic charm was tried.

The traditional religions of the world thus find themselves in an increasingly secular situation, and it is not surprising that they are beginning to examine one another's beliefs more carefully than they have done in the past. The figures below, which are only approximate, give a rough picture of the numerical strength of the major world religions today.

Some of them, like Buddhism, Christianity and Islam (or Mohammedanism) have always been missionary religions. They claim to be able to meet the needs of man the world over, irrespective of his race or nationality, or the colour of his skin. Since the end of the Second World War two of these religions, Buddhism and Islam, have shown signs of greatly increased vigour and activity. The same has also been true of Hinduism, which is not usually thought of as a missionary religion. This religious revival has gone hand in hand with the reaction of the peoples of India, the Far East and Africa against the domination of the West. It has made them increasingly critical of Christianity as a mainly "Western" religion, and turned them back with fresh interest to their own religious traditions. Today Buddhists and Mohammedans are looking towards the Western nations as a possible mission field, and books about Buddhism and Islam are being specially written with Western readers in mind.

Some religions are, on principle, not missionary in outlook, and one of these is Judaism. The Jews have always believed that they stand in a special relationship with God and that those people who are not born into the Jewish faith cannot completely share in it. For this reason they have not tried to make converts and as a result their religion has not spread as much as some others.

Down the years Jewish people have made an immense contribution to science, to art, to music and to culture generally. Jews have been active in the worlds of politics, philosophy, industry and commerce. They have been among the world's greatest financiers. Their reverence for home and family life has meant that problems of crime and juvenile delinquency are largely unknown amongst them. And within Christianity itself, the fact that Jesus was himself a Jew, and that in a very real sense the New Testament grew out of the Old, compels us to pay tribute to their traditions and culture. Yet despite all this, antisemitism (or persecution of the Jews) has been one of the world's recurrent problems since the Middle Ages.

CHRISTIANITY AND OTHER RELIGIONS

STATISTICS OF SOME OF THE WORLD'S RELIGIONS (in millions)

	100	200	300	400	500	600	700	800	900
Sikhs	6m								
Jews	12m								
Shintoists	35m								
African Tribal Religions	50m								
Buddhists			300m						
Confucians and Taoists			300m						
Hindus				366m					
Moslems				400m					
Christians									940m

It has shown itself in one form or another in practically every nation where Jewish people have settled down to live. Worst of all, it springs from the fact that Christians throughout their history have blamed the Jews for the crucifixion of Jesus Christ.

Antisemitism can break out almost any time, anywhere. In 1967, for instance, when it became known that actors from Oberammergau and Thiersee were going on tour in Britain to present the Passion Play, the Jewish authorities became anxious in case any "incidents" occurred. Fortunately all the performances passed off smoothly.

As everyone knows, antisemitism reached its peak with the mass persecution of Jews in Nazi Germany, and no-one can read Anne Frank's diary or visit the Frank house in Amsterdam without being reminded of the horror of those nightmare days. Hitler's "solution" to the Jewish problem included the extermination of every Jewish person in Germany, and as news of the concentration camps and the gas chambers filtered through to wartime Britain, concern grew. Many religious leaders felt the need for an organisation which would work to combat racial and religious intolerance and to check the spread of any antisemitic movement in Britain. And so, in 1942, with bombs falling on Britain, the Council of Christians and Jews came into being. Its life began officially on October 1st of that year with an announcement in *The Times* stating that its objects were :

'To combat all forms of religious and racial intolerance. To promote mutual understanding and goodwill between Christians and Jews, and to foster co-operation in educational activities and in social and community service.'

During the war years, for obvious reasons, progress was slow, but once it was over the pace quickened considerably. In 1946 the first International Conference of Christians and Jews was held at Oxford, and similar gatherings continue to be a feature of the Council's work. In 1952 the Queen became Patron of the Council and in 1967, on the 25th Anniversary of its formation, she and the Duke of Edinburgh attended a Jubilee celebration concert.

Since the early wartime days branches of the Council have been set up in many parts of Britain. Work among young people has been developed and International Youth Conferences are now regularly held. Lectures, brains trusts and discussions are arranged, and the Council directs a part of its work especially towards schools. It works also through the printed word, and its quarterly journal, "Common Ground", contains articles written by both Christians and Jews on matters of common interest to all.

In 1966, as part of the 900th Anniversary celebrations at Westminster Abbey, the Council arranged an exhibition. Entitled "The Corner of the Earth" it covered many aspects of Jewish history and ritual, and was much appreciated by those of other beliefs who came to see it.

Because Jews and Christians share a common heritage, the work of the Council of Christians and Jews has been easier than it otherwise might have been. The contacts which have been established in Britain are valuable, but they are only a first step in the much greater task of forging creative links with other world religions. If respect and tolerance towards one another's cherished beliefs can be shown, it should surely be possible to achieve this objective.

1. Is there a future for the work of Christian missionaries in today's shrinking world?
2. If it is possible, invite a practising Muslim or Jew to speak about his religion to your form.
3. Recommended reading: *A Book of World Religions* by E. G. Parrinder (Hulton Educational Publications, 1965).
4. Make notes on *one* non-Christian religion and then prepare a booklet containing information and illustrations about it.

35   SEX AND MARRIAGE

Ask any group of teenagers to write down on a piece of paper what they worry most about, and there is little doubt that for most of them it will be sex. Ask them to say what subject interests them most, and they will probably give the same answer. Yet whilst advertisements on television and elsewhere stress the importance of sex in a variety of ways, parents and older people often seem reluctant or unable to advise young people about it. Most churches, and many ministers, seem to dodge discussion of it. And other teenagers, if we ask them, usually seem to think of it as something to be joked about or sniggered at.

At the Mayflower Family Centre in London the teenagers ask all the usual questions. "Is intercourse outside marriage wrong ? " "What about contraceptives ? " "How far should a Christian go with his girl-friend ? " "How can you know what's right and wrong in sex ? "

Sex is dynamite and David Sheppard likes his young people to realise it. "With any powerful machine," he says, "the maker gives his instructions for its use, as it can be dangerous if misused."

And so at the Mayflower, in the discussions on sex, teenagers learn something about the less romantic side of the subject. At one session, for instance, they had been reading about an ordinary week's work in the life of one of London's leading doctors, a gynaecologist in a hospital. A grim tale unfolded as he told of thirteen unwanted pregnancies, one girl mentally ill through attempting to procure a miscarriage, and two illegal abortions. "These cases are not exceptional," he had written, "It is the same every week."

To some of those Mayflower teenagers these facts came as a shock. They feel strongly that parents owe it to their children to answer questions about sex as truthfully and honestly as they can.

Often in their group discussions at the Mayflower they go back to some of the things Jesus had to say on the subject of sex and marriage. His words, for example, in the first verses of Matthew Chapter 19 show what he wanted a real marriage to be like. In this passage he emphasises that the feelings which a boy and girl have for each other are put there by God — and therefore completely healthy. And he goes on to show that a true marriage is for keeps — a union for life — and that its claims are superior even to the claims of parents.

The other incident they often consider is at the beginning of Chapter 8 in John's Gospel. This tells how a woman, caught in the very act of committing adultery, is brought to Jesus by the Scribes and Pharisees. The Old Testament law decreed that such women should be stoned to death, and Christ's questioners meant to trick him by asking what he thought about her.

Jesus deals with the problem in two parts. First of all, he shows a wonderful understanding of how men's minds work! He challenges any man in the group around him who has not at some time wanted to commit adultery to be the first to throw a stone at the woman. And then, when the men, one by one, have all slunk away, he speaks to the woman herself. To her, two things are made quite clear. First, Jesus does not condemn her for what she has done. Second, he does not condone her sin, and he tells her "Go home, and do not sin again."

The girls at the Mayflower see this story as one example of how Christ worked all the time to give women and girls a new status and dignity in society — and nearly all the young people are surprised to discover how positive Jesus is on the topic of sex, especially since the Church so often seems to say 'no' to most of the questions connected with it.

Though it makes it quite clear that intercourse outside marriage is wrong, the Bible does not give a direct answer to all the problems. Many of them have to be resolved personally by the young people who ask them. Yet so far as the boys are concerned, David Sheppard finds that many sex questions become easier to answer when a young man has first answered the question "Is my girl-friend a person — or a plaything?" From that point, many a young person can be shown that there is more in the love of a man and woman than just strong physical attraction. Though that is of great importance, another kind of love (which we can call "caring") is necessary too. This is the kind of love which holds two people together when, for one reason or another, sex takes a holiday. It is the kind of love which makes you ask "What am I giving?" instead of "What am I getting?" It is the kind of love Christ died to show to the world.

Certainly those young people at the Mayflower Family Centre who are trying to follow Christ in their daily lives day by day find a difference in their courtships. Their faith has given them a new respect for each other as persons. Because of that, it has brought a new respect for each other physically as well.

Some of those Christian young people, as we saw last term,

have been getting married and settling down to live near to the Mayflower in Canning Town. From time to time they have opened their homes up to a group from the Centre for an evening's discussion. They have talked frankly about the problems and the difficulties of married life. They have been equally frank about their faith in Jesus Christ. True, it has not made saints of them and they would be the first to admit it. But they have been able to show how it has given them added patience and understanding with one another, especially during the first difficult and trying months of married life.

Many of those who have listened, their marriages still ahead of them, have later decided to follow their example.

1. Examine the advertisements on television or in a glossy magazine. Do you think some of them appeal to "wrong" instincts in the reader? If so, say why.
2. Recommended reading: *Young People and Sex* by Julia Dawkins —No. 19 in *Thinking Things Through* (S.C.M. Press Ltd.); *Loving* by David Sheppard (Scripture Union Press 1966).
3. Do you think instruction in sex should be given in every secondary school? If so, by whom?
4. Discuss divorce. Should divorce be made easier to obtain or more difficult?
5. Do you think the trend towards earlier marriages is a good thing, or are there dangers in marrying early?

Apart from marriage, the change from school to work is the greatest in which most young people are ever involved. From the fairly sheltered environment of school, with its varied programme and short day, teenagers often move to longer hours spent on repetitive work which is not aimed primarily at pleasing young employees! As a young apprentice fitter once put it "At school you are more or less looked after by the teachers and you are with your own companions. When you go to work you are the lad in the shop, fetching the tea, sweeping up, and cleaning the benches." He added later "Some days I feel I've really got a share in a big organisation and at other times I go inside the works and I just become a number, pushed around by other people, and that's not good."

The workers of our country today, at $25\frac{1}{2}$ million, represent less than half the total population. Two thirds are men. On average, each of these men works 47.7 hours per week. Astonishingly, this figure is almost exactly what it was before the war in 1938. What has changed is our situation with regard to overtime working, for Britain now works more overtime than any other country except France. It's a sobering thought, then, that an Englishman today spends about $42\frac{1}{2}$ per cent of his waking hours at work. Put like that, the choice of a job is a very important one. Yet it is surprising how many people seem to be miserable at work — and how many more would say that their real life begins when they 'clock out' of the factory or office each evening.

More and more girls, too, are continuing to work after they get married. With a longer expectation of life and earlier marriage, a woman can often look forward to a working life of twenty years even after her children have grown up. Nearly all the careers and professions are now open to women, and equality between the two sexes is closer today than it has ever been before in history.

At the Mayflower Centre in East London young people often argue about the subject of work. Many of the members of the club earn their living by working with their hands, and some of them are ambitious. Already they know what is meant by the term "the rat race" — and some of them would admit to being caught up in it. Often they put a question such as this : 'Some Christians seem to think it's wrong to have ambitions. Surely it must be right to want to get on ? ' Frequently they are surprised by the sort of reply they get from their leaders. A good deal of what Jesus said seems to cut right across the business of getting on in the world and achieving material success. They press hard for concrete examples from the Bible, and the parable in Luke Chapter 12 (verses 16—21) illustrates the point. In this story, a rich man's crops were so heavy one year that at harvest-time he had to build even bigger barns in which to store them away for the winter. But it was obvious that though his material wealth was very great, he was a bankrupt spiritually. He had been so busy 'building up' and 'getting on' that he had lived entirely selfishly and without thought of anyone but himself.

Another well known story is also specific about the matter of wealth. In Matthew Chapter 19 (verses 16—24) a young man comes to Jesus. He wants to know what he must do in order to secure the 'eternal life' which Christ was so often talking about. When Jesus tells him that he must keep the commandments he is able, without any priggishness, to reply that his life has been based on them since his very youngest days. Where, then, does he still fall short ? Jesus replies that if he wants to be perfect he must sell all his possessions and give the proceeds to poor people. We are told that he went away sad, because he was very rich.

These references to the Bible sparked off a lively response from the group. Did all this mean that money was in itself evil, someone wanted to know ? One of the boys came in, "No, it doesn't. But it does mean a very serious state of affairs for anyone who gets to the stage where money is the master of his life, instead of his servant." The group went on talking for a long time about money. One of them had been working overtime voluntarily most weekends — and doing electrical odd jobs in people's homes several evenings a week — in order to buy extra things for the flat in which he lived with his wife and baby boy. The group was sharply divided about this. Some felt it was inevitable that this sort of thing should happen whilst a couple were building up their home. Others believed, just as strongly, that excessive overtime can throw life out of balance

for the whole family, and can be dangerous for the future of the marriage as well.

The conversation swung back to the original question about ambition and wanting to get on. At this point David Sheppard joined in the discussion. "Of course promotion, a new job, more money and perhaps a fresh environment as well may all be in God's plan for one person" he told them. "But it's just as likely that the plan for someone else may say, 'Stay where you are in your present job, and be a good influence on your workmates there.' My belief," he concluded, "is that we should stay where we are unless we are quite sure God wants us to move on elsewhere." As we have already seen, some of the young married couples in Canning Town have taken this advice to heart so far as setting up house is concerned.

The group went on to discuss the reasons for work. Some of them said quite frankly that they found work a dull, boring routine, lacking any real "drive" or sense of purpose. They could understand a parson, or even a Christian nurse or teacher feeling that they were on full-time duty for Jesus Christ, but what about a person whose work is monotonous or repetitive ? It was agreed that there is a small proportion of jobs so monotonous that it is practically impossible to take any real pride in doing them — and the sooner a machine can be found to do them the better ! But for the rest of us, it should certainly be possible to take a much higher view of our work than we commonly do.

Whenever the group talks about work, there always seems to be a pile of questions and problems to be discussed and answered. Certainly this topic never gets "used up". They have argued about whether or not to join a Trade Union (there are over 600 in this country today with nearly ten million members!) They have discussed "scrounging" or "knocking off". Many of them have put their boss under the microscope. And still the questions come ! It's a big subject, this business of trying to be a Christian in the place where you work !

1. Read Mark 8 v. 36.
    (a) Would you advise a man to give up his job if you believed him to be in this sort of danger?
    (b) Are there some jobs you would *not* do—however highly you were paid?
2. "We can hardly respect money enough for the blood and toil it represents. Money is frightening. It can serve or destroy man." (from *Prayer before a Five Pound Note* by Michael Quoist). Discuss this.
3. "No pop-singer or film star is worth a salary hundreds of times bigger than that of a nurse or a doctor." Is this "sour grapes" or common sense?
4. Is it impossible to be a Christian in industry?
5. Write down some of the things which you are most looking forward to when you start work. Do you think you will ever become the sort of person whose only interest is in the wage or salary the job provides?

37   TIME ON YOUR HANDS

Twenty or thirty years ago the first washing machines and electric irons began to change the lives of some hard-worked house-wives. Today, the process is much farther advanced, and we are in the computer age. Not only have today's machines revolutionised life in the kitchen : they have also taken over some of the jobs by which, up to now, men and women have earned their living for forty or more hours a week. It seems almost certain that within the lifetime of young people who read this book, a twelve hour working week will become possible. And that means a great deal more time to do what we like with — a great deal more leisure.

And yet it's surprising how many people dread having more time on their hands. Business men, for example, often seem to go to pieces when they retire. They find it difficult to fill their leisure hours, and life becomes rather a burden.

At the Mayflower Family Centre the teenagers find that working out how to spend one's spare time is not just an old person's problem. Some of them are apprentices, and they enjoy their jobs tremendously. They find that their minds are stretched and stimulated by their work because they are constantly learning new things and facing new challenges. By contrast, they are frequently bored by some of the things they do with their leisure. And when they come to analyse it, many of them admit that this is because what they do in their spare time is generally entirely for their own pleasure.

Most of these teenagers in Canning Town, East London, would agree that they are happiest when they have a plan of action, or "programme", which includes not only work but leisure time as well. And this would probably be true for most of us. Of course, if we have been working especially hard for weeks or months on end we long for the chance to be completely lazy for a while and do nothing. But when the break actually comes, a day or two's idleness is usually enough — and then we are ready once again to *do* something. In a society like ours, of course, it should be everyone's right to choose for himself how to spend his free time. Yet the outlook and views of other people are often interesting, and so sometimes at the Mayflower the youngsters consider passages such as the two below in order to get another point of view. On both occasions the speaker is Jean-Baptiste Clamence, the chief character in a modern play by Albert Camus called *The Fall*:

"I never cross a bridge at night. It's because of a vow. Suppose, after all, that someone should jump in the water. One of two things— either you follow suit to fish him out and, in cold weather, that's taking a great risk! Or you forsake him there and to suppress the dive sometimes leaves a great aching."

"When I see a new face, something inside me sounds the alarm. 'Slow! Danger!' Even when the attraction is strongest I am on my guard."

Clamence is like a good many people today. In his daily work he is probably forced to rub shoulders with people he doesn't like, and often he will accept this state of affairs simply because his job depends on it. But outside work — and in his leisure time especially — he doesn't want to be 'tied up'. He sees involvement with people as a threat to his independence. And so, as often as possible, he keeps strangers at arm's length.

Of course the Mayflower is the sort of place where it is impossible not to get mixed up with other people — you don't go again unless you are willing to be "involved". And David Sheppard believes that every church — and every Christian — should be prepared for this. Often he reads over with his young people the story Jesus told in Matthew Chapter 25 (verses 31—46). The division which is made there between those who were prepared to be involved with others and those who were not shows that Jesus had strong views on the use a man or woman makes of leisure. Christ has been called 'The Man for Others', and His second great commandment 'Love thy neighbour' bears this out. Certainly if we are making a list of the things Christianity includes we shall have to put in "Involvement".

At the Mayflower Church many people, old as well as young, have undertaken to visit regularly at least one person who finds it difficult to get about. Many of these calls, though by no means all, are to elderly people, and of course many of those who are visited have never been inside The Mayflower. There are days in spring and summer when certain of these people can get out if someone with a car will spare the time to take them for a run. And of course that can include an occasional trip to Church for those who want to go.

It would be quite wrong to think, however, that the youngsters down at The Mayflower are merely a crowd of "do-gooders" whose leisure begins and ends with wallpapering old people's bedrooms or singing a hymn or two round a hospital bed. As often as possible they like to be together, and so frequently they will crowd into their club leader's flat and listen for a while to records. Then the record player is switched off and, with some sitting on the floor and some standing, a discussion begins. Often Christian subjects and problems are discussed, and different points of view expressed, and several will speak from their own experience about how Christ can make a difference to daily living. Sometimes the group gets an invitation to spend the evening in the house or flat where a young couple have recently set up home together. These sessions are especially valuable because they are a chance to show whether Christian belief and faith are effective for the early, testing months of married life. There are several couples in Canning Town who believe that it is!

Certainly The Mayflower young people rarely suffer from boredom or loneliness. Perhaps this comes about because, having declared war on other people's loneliness they have solved the problem of their own.

————◆————

1. More than 85% of all households in this country now have television. Are any of the following opinions a fair description of its present influence in Britain?
   (a) "It's a crime university."
   (b) "T.V. empties full lives."
   (c) "It fills empty lives."
2. "Never be triflingly employed." (John Wesley to his helpers.) Do you think this is useful advice for young people of the present generation?
3. Imagine that the twelve hour working week has become a reality, and that you are happily married with a young family. How would you spend your leisure time?

38   NO PLACE LIKE HOME

There's still a serious housing shortage in Britain. It isn't just an imaginary problem, as one mythical Cabinet Minister is supposed to have said, dreamed up by people who have nowhere to live! Despite the fact that we build over 400,000 houses each year in this country, we still need many more.

As these new houses are put up, people of all sorts move into them. Some are young couples, setting up for the first time, and leaving the old family "nest" behind them. Some are families, perhaps re-housed from overcrowded accommodation or from old, decaying property in a depressed area. Some are old people, often widows or widowers, no longer able to look after themselves in a large house and now moving into an old person's bungalow or maisonette.

NO PLACE LIKE HOME

One of the best things about a new house is that when people move in they usually exchange something rather dark and drab for a light, airy place where everything seems bright. And very often that makes them want to take extra trouble to keep it that way. If they are able to do so they will probably buy some new furniture and curtains. Dad's life may soon begin to revolve round decorating and "Do it Yourself", whilst Mum will revel in keeping everything spick and span. From this point, however, it is only a short step to the situation where a house becomes, not a home, but a show-piece. The Home-god then becomes a real danger.

A great deal of change in housing has been going on in London's East End since the war. Most homes contain at least some of the most important modern "gadgets" and it is good to see a car standing outside many of them. Slums are disappearing fast and new accommodation is rising in their place. In many places vast blocks of flats have replaced the old "back to backs" and they tower over Canning Town like so many cliffs in the sky.

Yet David Sheppard, Warden of The Mayflower, finds that despite these welcome changes some of the good features from the old days seem to have been lost. "The old rows of terraced houses may have seemed all dustbins and rickety doors," he says, "but there was a great deal of friendliness on the doorsteps, and the neighbours rallied round whenever there was a need to help. It is not so easy to have such a free relationship in a fifteen storey block of flats."

In their group discussions the Mayflower teenagers confirm this. There are nicer rooms in most homes today, but the neighbours are not asked in as often as once they were. Greater prosperity seems to have led to greater independence, and the attitude of "We stand on our own feet" can often mean "We don't want help from anyone — not even God! "

Of course it is possible for a family to become self-sufficient like this almost without realising it. It is very easy for a father's prayer (if he ever says one) to become quite simply "God bless me and my wife; and my son John and his wife." And not many people realise that if you love only your own family you are really loving yourself. As Jesus puts it (in Luke Chapter 6 and verse 32) "If you love only those who love you, what credit is that to you ? Even sinners love

156

those who love them ! " Of course this does not mean that we are to stop loving wives, or children or parents. Of course it is quite true that "Charity begins at home". But charity need not, and should not, stop there. God's love is not rationed.

Just as there are homes where love seems limited to the immediate family, so there are many where it does not seem ever to have reached the children. One East End teenager, for instance, put it like this : "What do I remember about Mum and Dad ? Well, it was always a case of 'Here you are, son. Half-a-crown for the pictures : don't get into trouble . . . ' I saw a little kid the other day," he went on. "He kept wanting to tell his Mum something. She was on the gossip with a couple of pram-pushers. She didn't even notice him tugging at her hand." Then he paused for a moment "If you ask me," he said, "God's a million miles away. He couldn't be interested in me. Who'd miss me, anyway ? You tell me that."

That boy from Canning Town is like many others. He is not going to believe that God cares for him unless first he sees that other people are concerned for him. Every young person with the love and care of parents behind him and something steady to live for should stop and think about lads like this. So should every adult.

The row that sixteen year old Jean had with her parents was typical of what happens in many families as teenagers grow up. It was nobody's fault really. Father wanted to book up at Margate for the annual August holiday as usual. Jean wanted to go away with her boy-friend and another young couple. Her brother Jack, who was only twenty, was getting married in the September and wasn't able to afford a holiday plus a honeymoon as well. Dad accused Jean of not wanting to spend time with her parents and then added straight away that he just hadn't the money to let her go away on holiday with Ken. Then Jean flared back at him. The real reason, she said, was that neither of her parents really liked Ken, or, for that matter, ever had.

The fact is that there are "mixed up" parents as well as "mixed up" teenagers. Jean's parents were about to experience a big upheaval in their family life — and frankly they were dreading it. They longed for a real, trusting relationship with Jean and Jack. Yet they did not realise that the foundations for it should have been laid in the years when the children were very young. If a breakdown in communication between children and their parents is to be avoided in the teenage years, planning must begin early.

Many of the couples at The Mayflower who are now married and bringing up young families in Canning Town are realising the importance of all this. Despite the fact that the young mothers are all busy housewives as well, many of them find time to pray during their busy day — not with hands folded and eyes closed necessarily — but in the middle of the routine of the home. "God among the dishes", one of them calls it — and it's a centreing of their thoughts, perhaps only for a moment or two, on other people and *their* needs, as well as upon God. Their husbands, at work somewhere in a factory, office or workshop, will be trying to do the same thing under equally difficult conditions. And at the end of the day they will often compare notes. Being Christians, these young parents know that the real challenge to living is not how we manage on Sundays, but how we live at home and at work seven days of the week.

---

1. Using a modern translation, read Matthew Chapter 10 from verse 34 to the end of the chapter. What do you think Jesus intends us to learn from the things he said in this passage?
2. Do you consider that the moves towards a "freer" Sunday are a threat to home and family life in this country?
3. "The family that prays together, stays together." Do you think a revival of the old custom of family prayers would help to make home life today more stable?"

USEFUL ADDRESSES

Alcoholics Anonymous, 11 Redcliffe Gardens, London, S.W.10.

British and Foreign Bible Society, 146 Queen Victoria Street, London, E.C.4.

British Council of Churches, 10 Eaton Gate, London, S.W.1.

Campaign Against Racial Discrimination (CARD), 23 St. George's House, Toynbee Hall, Commercial Street, London, E.1.

Cheshire Foundation Homes for the Sick (See : The Mission for the Relief of Suffering).

Christian Aid, 10 Eaton Gate, London, S.W.1.

Churches Council on Gambling, The, 19 Abbey House, Victoria Street, London, S.W.1.

Community Service Volunteers, Toynbee Hall, 28 Commercial Street, London, E.1.

Council of Christians and Jews, 41 Cadogan Gardens, London, S.W.3.

Danilo Dolci Trust, 29 Great James Street, London, W.C.1.

Division of Inter Church Aid, Refugee and World Service, World Council of Churches, Geneva, Switzerland.

Friends of Vellore, The, Vellore House, Claverly Villas, Finchley, London, N.3.

Gamblers Anonymous, 19 Abbey House, Victoria Street, London, S.W.1.

Guide Dogs for the Blind Association, 83/89 Uxbridge Road, Ealing, London, W.5.

Iona Community, The, 214 Clyde Street, Glasgow, C.1.

King George's Jubilee Trust, 166 Piccadilly, London, W.1.

Mayflower Family Centre, The, Cooper Street, Canning Town, London. E.16.

Mission for the Relief of Suffering, The, 7 Market Mews, London, W.1.

National Association on Drug Addiction, 9 Anchorage Close, London, S.W.19.

National Committee for Commonwealth Immigrants (N.C.C.I.), 6 Tilney Street, London, W.1.

National Marriage Guidance Council, Queen Anne Street, London, W.1

159

National Society for Mentally Handicapped Children, 5 Bulstrode Street, London, W.1.

N.S.P.C.C., 1 Riding House Street, London, W.1.

Ockenden Venture, The, White Rose Lane, Woking, Surrey.

Oxfam, 274 Banbury Road, Oxford.

Salvation Army, The, Queen Victoria Street, London, E.C.4.

Shelter ; National Campaign for the Homeless, 86 The Strand, London. W.C.2.

Society for Autistic Children, 100 Wise Lane, Mill Hill, London, N.W.7.

United Nations Association of Great Britain and Northern Ireland, 25 Charles Street, London, W.1.

United Nations Information Centre, 14-15 Stratford Place, London, W.1.

Voluntary Service Overseas, 3 Hanover Street, London, W.1.

War on Want, 9 Madeley Road, London, W.5.

Wycliffe Bible Translators, Bletchingley Road, Merstham, Redhill, Surrey.